Bond 11+

Non-verbal Reasoning

Multiple-Choice Test 1

Read the following:

- Do not begin the test or open this booklet until told to do so.

- Work as quickly and as carefully as you can.

- Answers should be marked in the answer booklet provided, not in this test booklet.

- You may do rough working on a separate sheet of paper.

- If you make a mistake cross out the mistake and write the new answer clearly.

- Be careful to keep your place in the accompanying answer booklet.

- You will have 50 minutes to complete the test.

Text © Andrew Baines 2003

Original illustrations © Nelson Thornes Ltd 2003

The right of Andrew Baines to be identified as the author of this work has been asserted by him in acordance with the Copyright, Designs and Patents Act 1988.

Published in 2003 by:

Nelson Thornes Ltd, Delta Place, 27 Bath Road, CHELTENHAM, GL53 7TH, United Kingdom

01 02 03 04 05 / 10 9 8 7 6 5 4 3 2 1

A catalogue record for this book is available from the British Library

ISBN 0-7487-7329-0

Illustrations by Art Construction

Page make-up by AMR Ltd

Printed in Croatia by Zrinski

Nelson Thornes is a Wolters Kluwer company, and is not associated in any way with NFER-Nelson.

Section 1

Which pattern on the right completes the second pair in the same way as the first pair?

Example

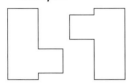 ?

a   b   c   (d)   e

Practice 1

   ?

a   b   c   d   e

Practice 2

   ?

  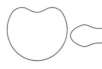

a   b   c   d   e

WAIT UNTIL YOU ARE TOLD TO GO ON

1 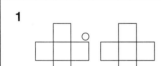 ?

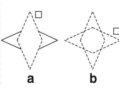 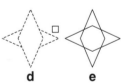

a   b   c   d   e

2   ?

a   b   c   d   e

3   ?

a   b   c   d   e

CONTINUE TO THE NEXT PAGE

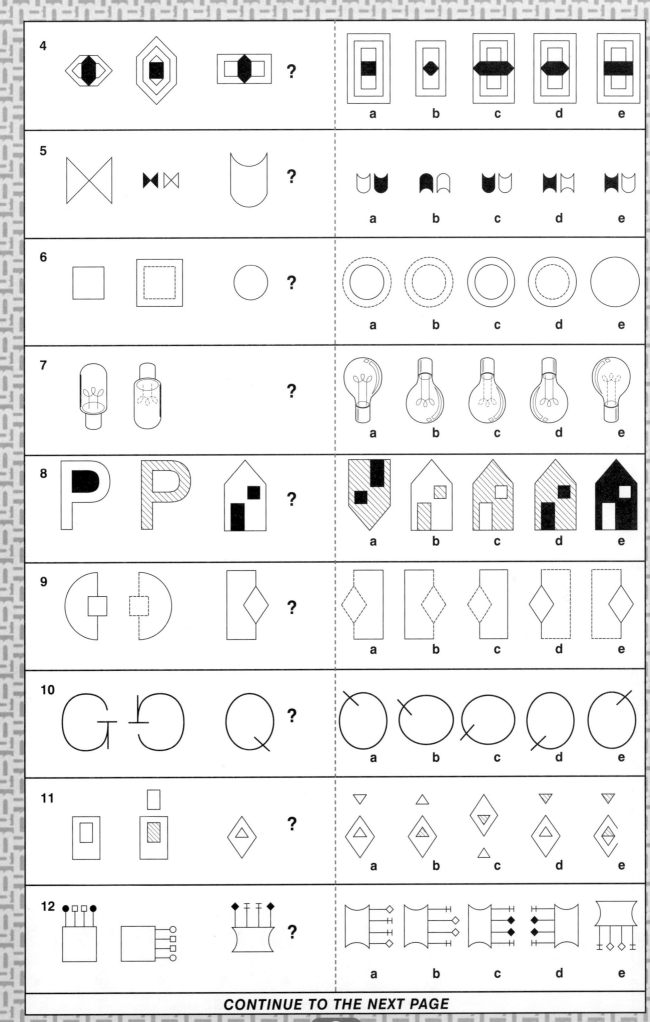

CONTINUE TO THE NEXT PAGE

Section 2

To the left of each row of shapes there are two shapes that are alike. Which pattern on the right belongs with the two on the left?

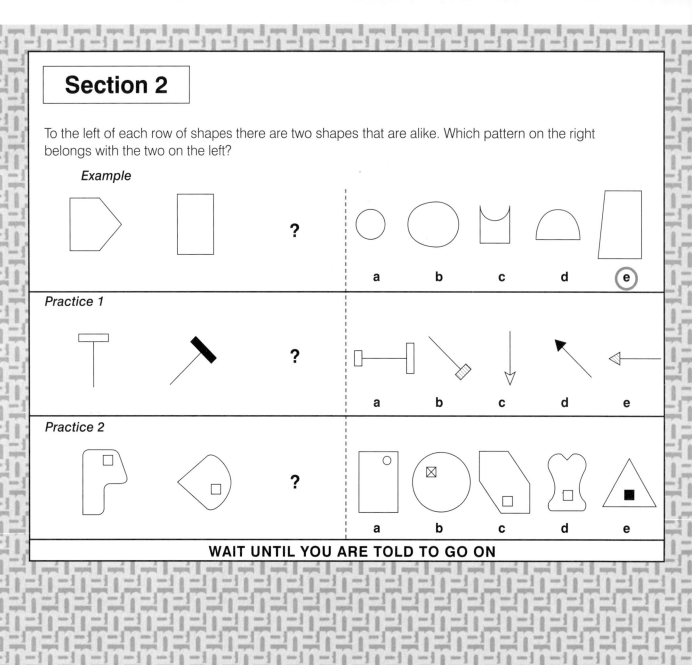

Example

a   b   c   d   e

Practice 1

a   b   c   d   e

Practice 2

a   b   c   d   e

WAIT UNTIL YOU ARE TOLD TO GO ON

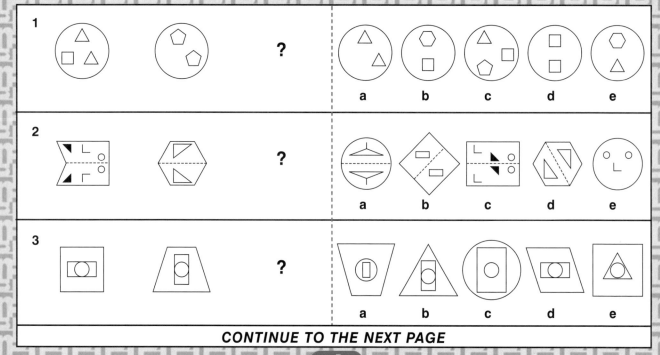

1

a   b   c   d   e

2

a   b   c   d   e

3

a   b   c   d   e

CONTINUE TO THE NEXT PAGE

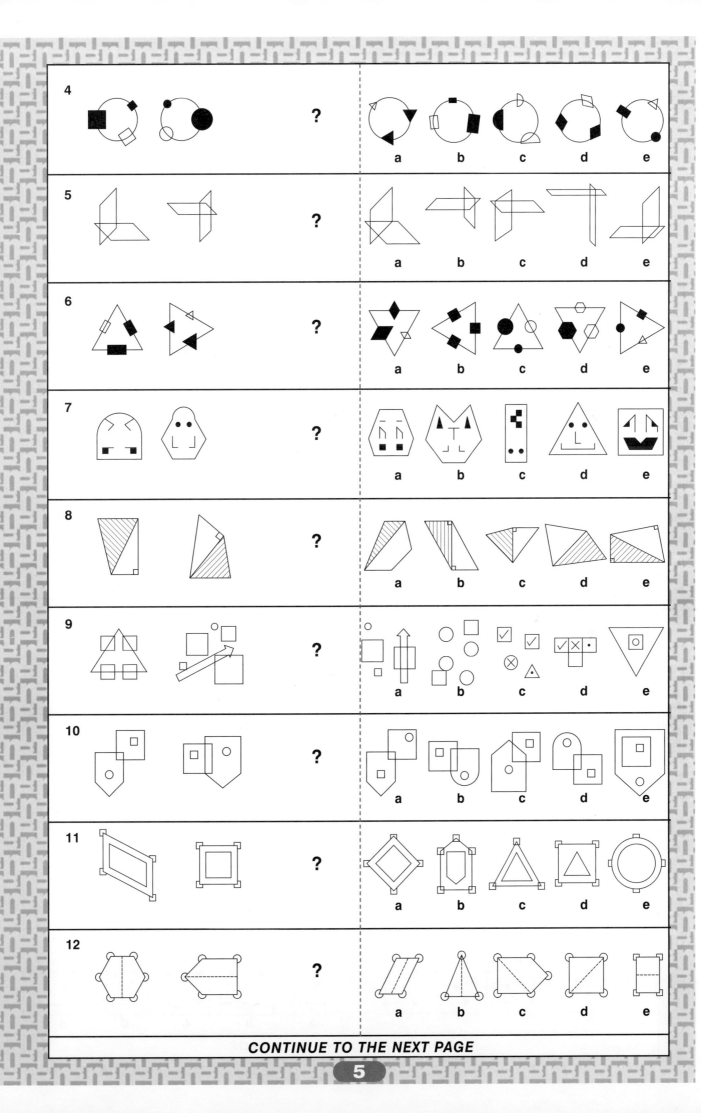

Section 3

The patterns below make a sequence. One pattern is missing. Which pattern completes the sequence?

Example

a b c d e

Practice 1

a b c d e

Practice 2

a b c d e

WAIT UNTIL YOU ARE TOLD TO GO ON

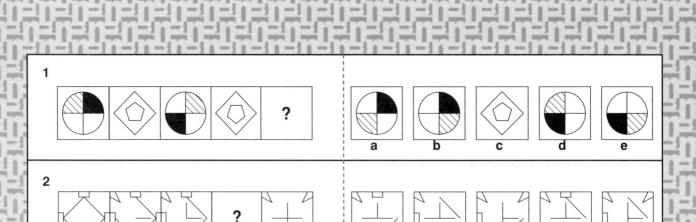

1   a b c d e

2   a b c d e

3   a b c d e

CONTINUE TO THE NEXT PAGE

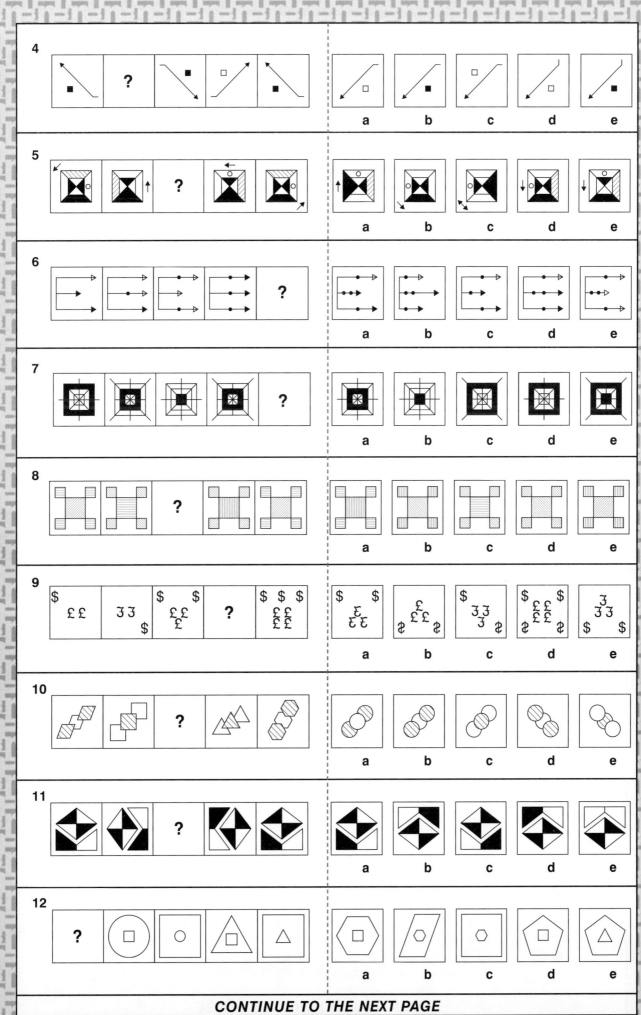

Section 4

Each of the patterns on the left has a two letter code. Select the correct code for the shape on the right following the same rules.

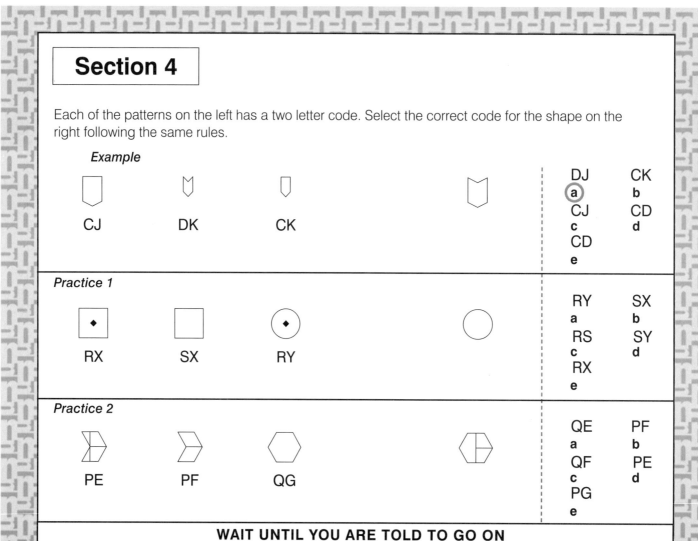

Example

CJ   DK   CK

DJ a
CJ c
CD e
CK b
CD d

Practice 1

RX   SX   RY

RY a
RS c
RX e
SX b
SY d

Practice 2

PE   PF   QG

QE a
QF c
PG e
PF b
PE d

WAIT UNTIL YOU ARE TOLD TO GO ON

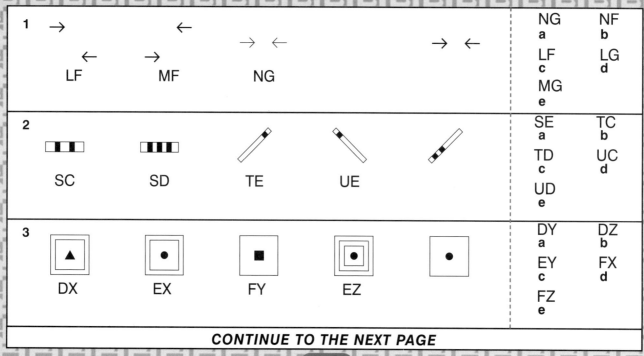

1
LF   MF   NG

NG a
LF c
MG e
NF b
LG d

2
SC   SD   TE   UE

SE a
TD c
UD e
TC b
UC d

3
DX   EX   FY   EZ

DY a
EY c
FZ e
DZ b
FX d

CONTINUE TO THE NEXT PAGE

8

4 AG AH BG

AH **a**	BG **b**
AG **c**	GH **d**
BH **e**	

5 SJ SJ TJ TK

TJ **a**	SJ **b**
TK **c**	JK **d**
SK **e**	

6 XL YM ZL

XM **a**	YM **b**
YL **c**	ZM **d**
XL **e**	

7 JR KR LS

LS **a**	JS **b**
LR **c**	KS **d**
JR **e**	

8 DR ES FR GS

DS **a**	ER **b**
FS **c**	GR **d**
FR **e**	

9 AN BO CO DP

BN **a**	BP **b**
CN **c**	CP **d**
DO **e**	

10 CF DF EG

CG **a**	DF **b**
DG **c**	EG **d**
EF **e**	

11 JR KS KT

JS **a**	JT **b**
KR **c**	KS **d**
JR **e**	

12 FS FT GT HU

FU **a**	GS **b**
GU **c**	HS **d**
HT **e**	

CONTINUE TO THE NEXT PAGE

Section 5

In the large square on the left one of the smaller squares is missing. Choose the shape or pattern that completes the square given.

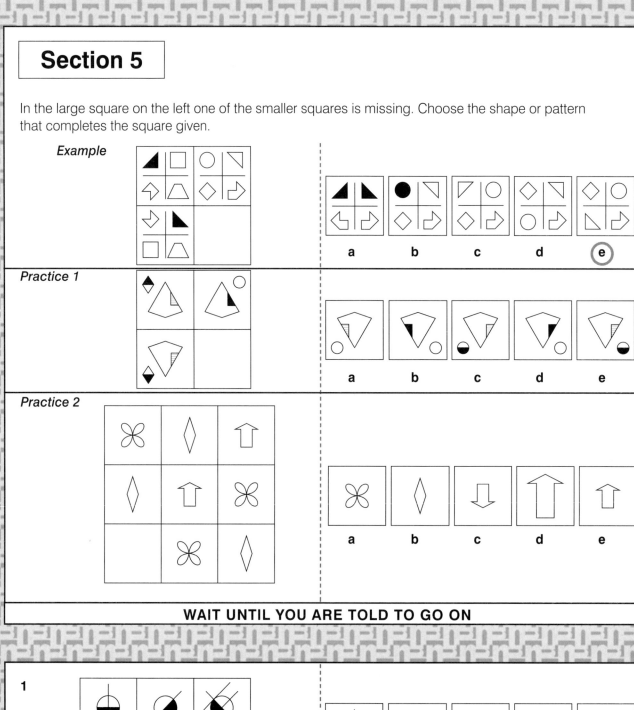

Example

a b c d (e)

Practice 1

a b c d e

Practice 2

a b c d e

WAIT UNTIL YOU ARE TOLD TO GO ON

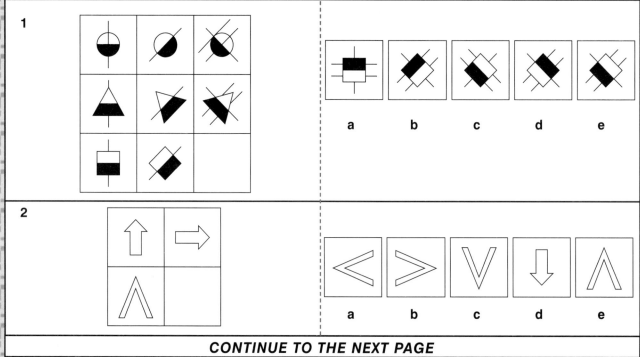

1

a b c d e

2

a b c d e

CONTINUE TO THE NEXT PAGE

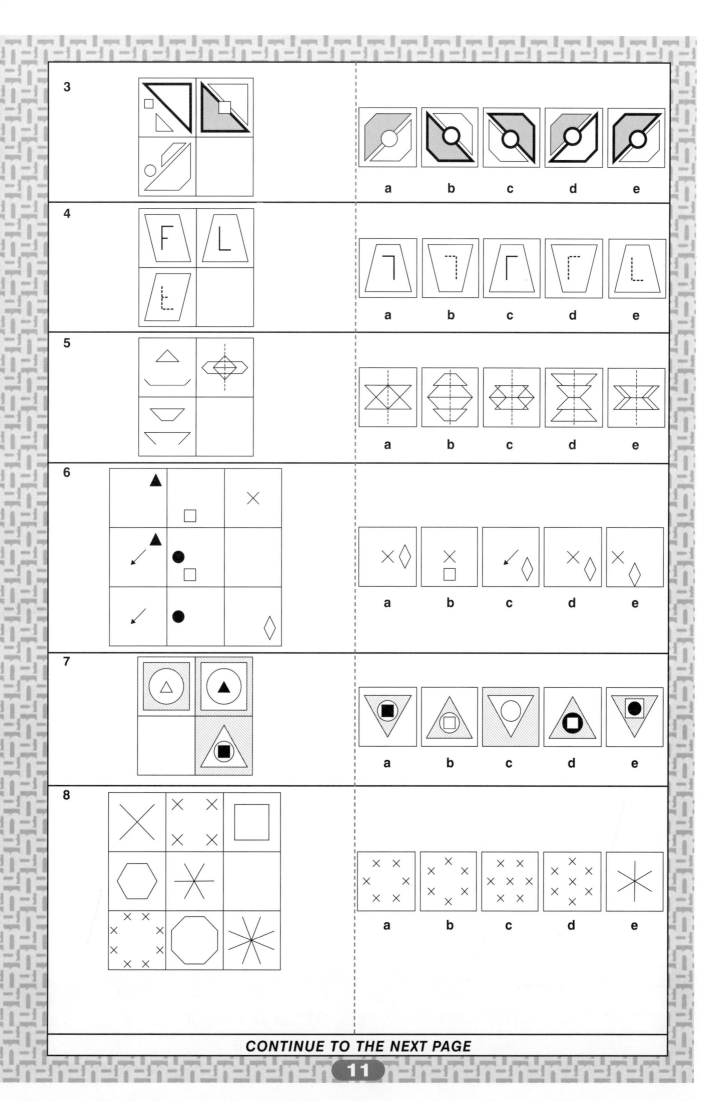

CONTINUE TO THE NEXT PAGE

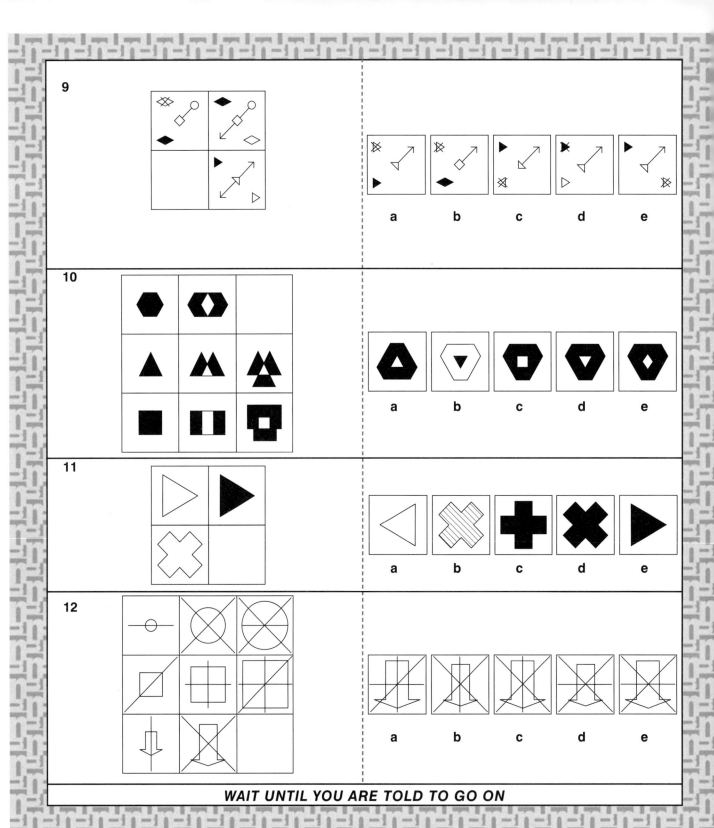

9

a b c d e

10

a b c d e

11

a b c d e

12

a b c d e

WAIT UNTIL YOU ARE TOLD TO GO ON

12

Bond 11+

Non-verbal Reasoning

Multiple-Choice Test 2

Read the following:

- Do not begin the test or open this booklet until told to do so.

- Work as quickly and as carefully as you can.

- Answers should be marked in the answer booklet provided, not in this test booklet.

- You may do rough working on a separate sheet of paper.

- If you make a mistake cross out the mistake and write the new answer clearly.

- Be careful to keep your place in the accompanying answer booklet.

- You will have 50 minutes to complete the test.

Text © Andrew Baines 2003

Original illustrations © Nelson Thornes Ltd 2003

The right of Andrew Baines to be identified as the author of this work has been asserted by him in acordance with the Copyright, Designs and Patents Act 1988.

All rights reserved, including translation. No part of this publication may be reproduced or transmitted in any form or by any means, electronic or mechanical, including photocopying, recording or duplication in any information storage and retrieval system, without permission in writing from the publisher or under licence from the Copyright Licensing Agency Ltd, of 90 Tottenham Court Road, London, W1T 4LP.

Any person who commits any unauthorised act in relation to this publication may be liable to criminal prosecution and civil claims for damages.

Published in 2003 by:

Nelson Thornes Ltd, Delta Place, 27 Bath Road, CHELTENHAM, GL53 7TH, United Kingdom

01 02 03 04 05 / 10 9 8 7 6 5 4 3 2 1

A catalogue record for this book is available from the British Library

ISBN 0-7487-7329-0

Illustrations by Art Construction

Page make-up by AMR Ltd

Printed in Croatia by Zrinski

Nelson Thornes is a Wolters Kluwer company, and is not associated in any way with NFER-Nelson.

Section 1

Which pattern on the right completes the second pair in the same way as the first pair?

Example

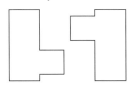 ?

a   b   c   ⓓ   e

Practice 1

   ?

a   b   c   d   e

Practice 2

   ?

a   b   c   d   e

WAIT UNTIL YOU ARE TOLD TO GO ON

---

1 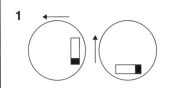 ?

a   b   c   d   e

2 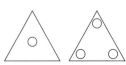 ?

 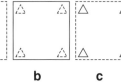 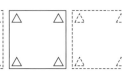

a   b   c   d   e

3   ?

  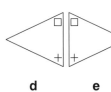

a   b   c   d   e

CONTINUE TO THE NEXT PAGE

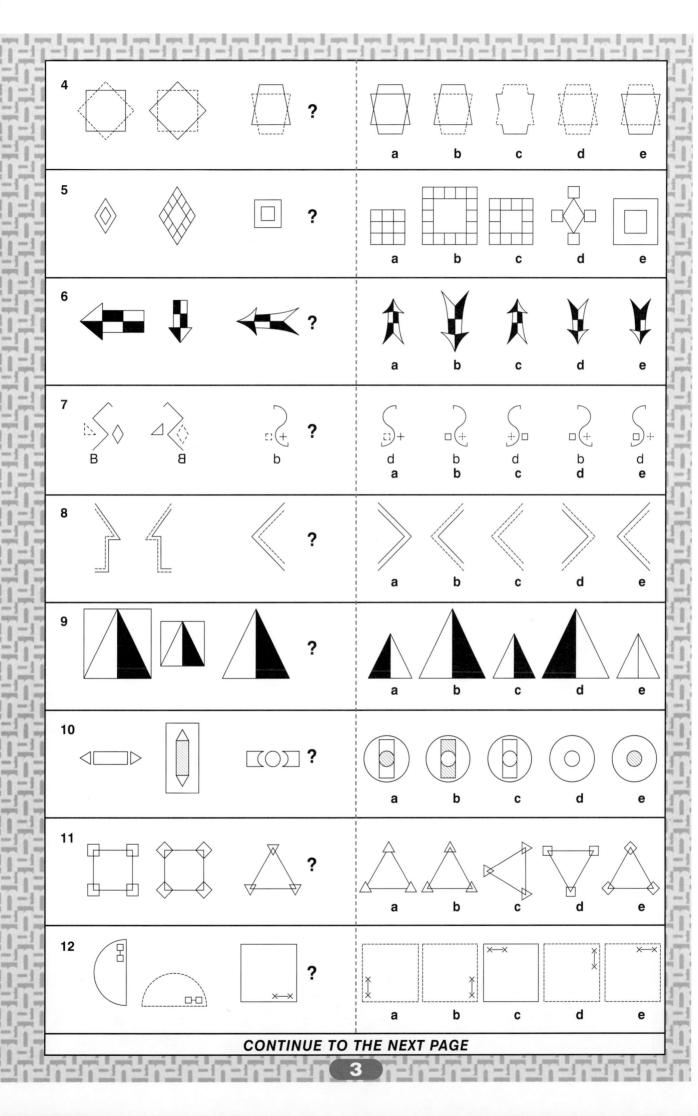

Section 2

To the left of each row of shapes there are two shapes that are alike. Which pattern on the right belongs with the two on the left?

Example

?

a b c d (e)

Practice 1

?

a b c d e

Practice 2

?

a b c d e

WAIT UNTIL YOU ARE TOLD TO GO ON

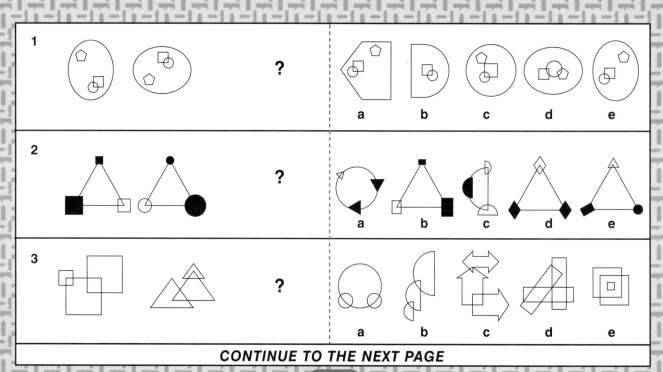

1 **?**

a b c d e

2 **?**

a b c d e

3 **?**

a b c d e

CONTINUE TO THE NEXT PAGE

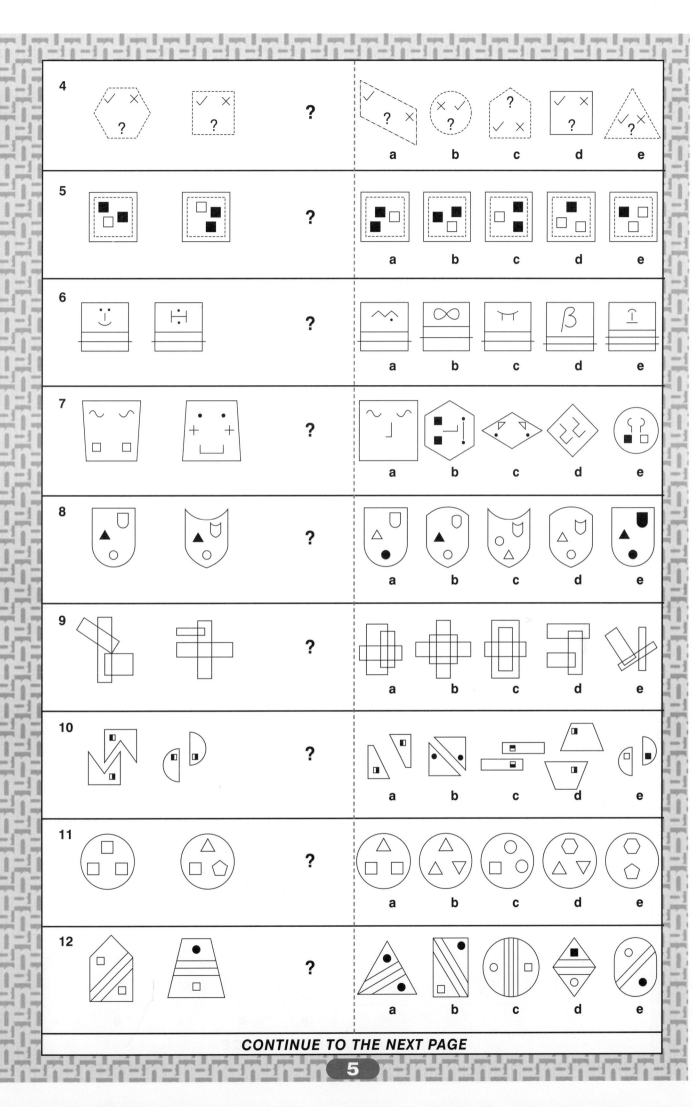

Section 3

The patterns below make a sequence. One pattern is missing. Which pattern completes the sequence?

Example

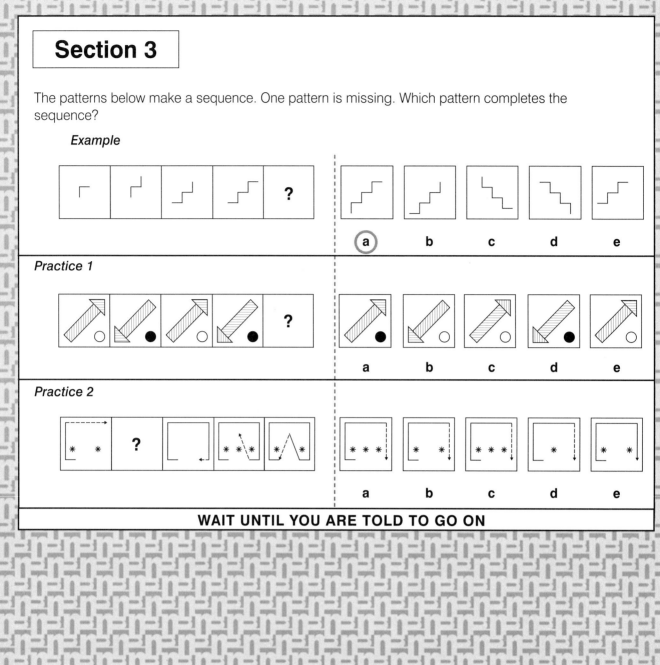

Practice 1

Practice 2

WAIT UNTIL YOU ARE TOLD TO GO ON

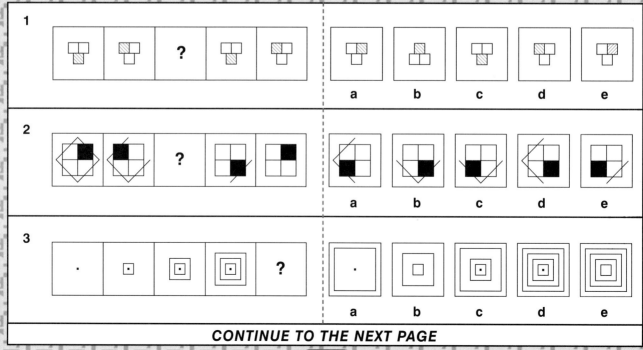

CONTINUE TO THE NEXT PAGE

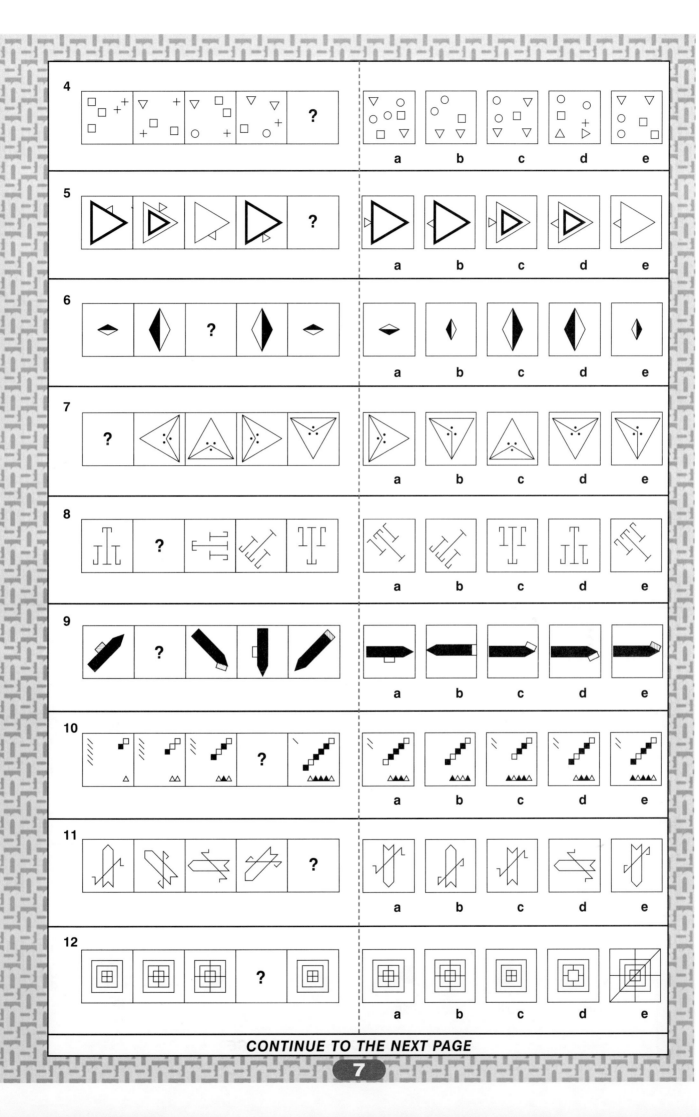

Section 4

Each of the patterns on the left has a two or three letter code. Select the correct code for the shape on the right following the same rules.

Example

				DJ	CK
				a	**b**
				CJ	CD
				c	**d**
				CD	
				e	
CJ	DK	CK			

Practice 1

				RY	SX
				a	**b**
				RS	SY
				c	**d**
				RX	
				e	
RX	SX	RY			

Practice 2

				QE	PF
				a	**b**
				QF	PE
				c	**d**
				PG	
				e	
PE	PF	QG			

WAIT UNTIL YOU ARE TOLD TO GO ON

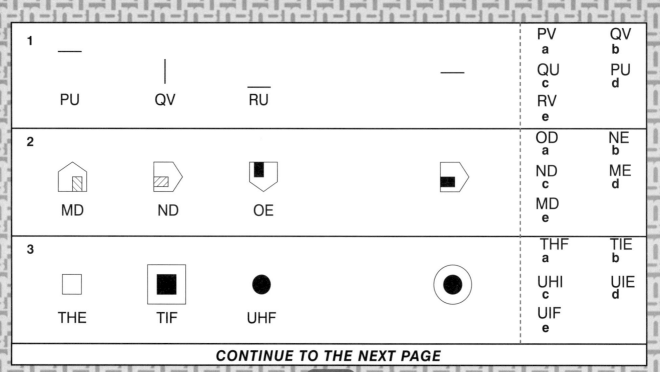

1

				PV	QV
				a	**b**
				QU	PU
				c	**d**
				RV	
				e	
PU	QV	RU			

2

				OD	NE
				a	**b**
				ND	ME
				c	**d**
				MD	
				e	
MD	ND	OE			

3

				THF	TIE
				a	**b**
				UHI	UIE
				c	**d**
				UIF	
				e	
THE	TIF	UHF			

CONTINUE TO THE NEXT PAGE

8

4

IT
JU
KV
KW

IV **a** JT **b**
JW **c** KT **d**
KV **e**

5

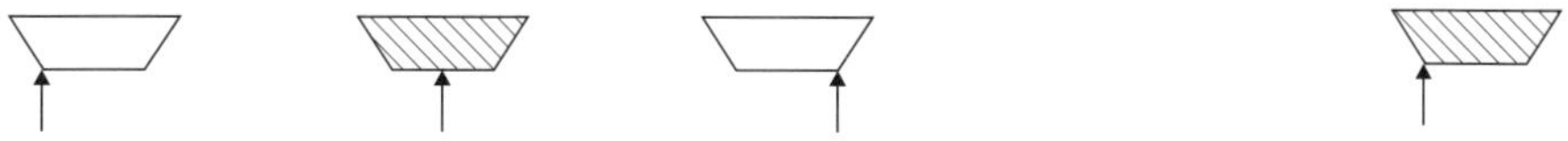
SM
TN
SO

TO **a** SN **b**
SM **c** SO **d**
TM **e**

6

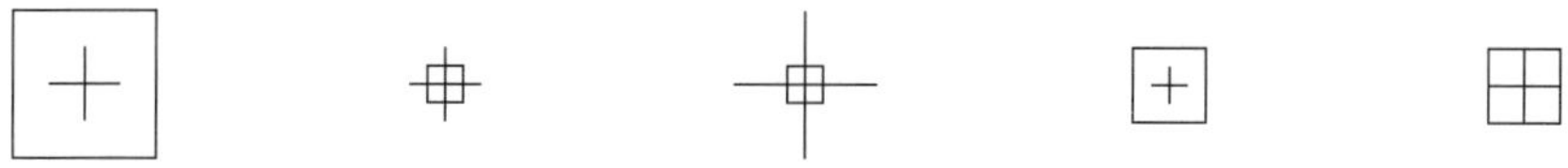
TG
TH
UH
VI

TI **a** UG **b**
UI **c** VG **d**
VH **e**

7

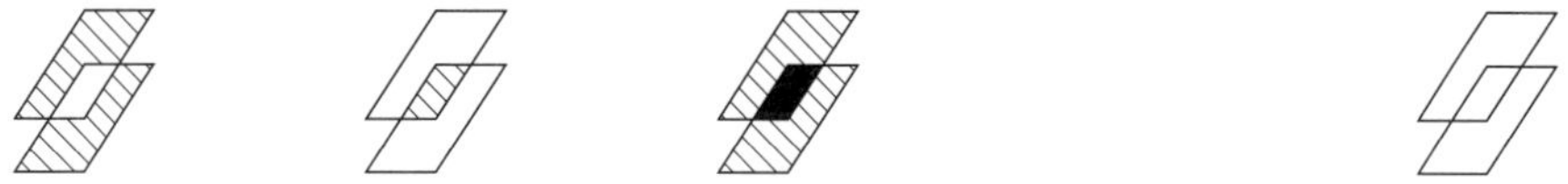
GP
HQ
GR

GQ **a** HR **b**
HQ **c** HP **d**
GP **e**

8

HV
IW
JW

HW **a** IV **b**
IW **c** JV **d**
HV **e**

9

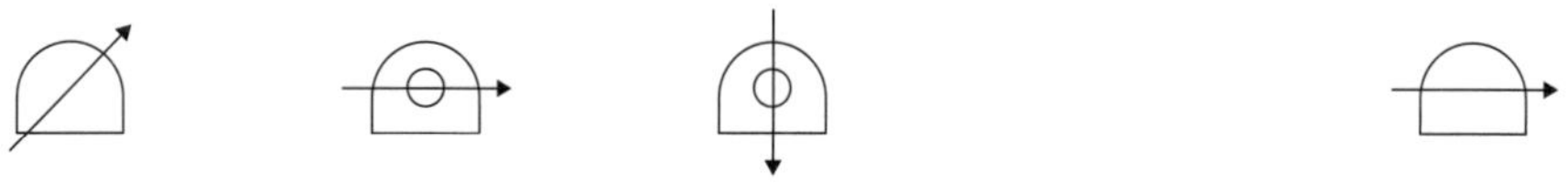
DN
EO
EP

DP **a** EO **b**
DO **c** EP **d**
EN **e**

10

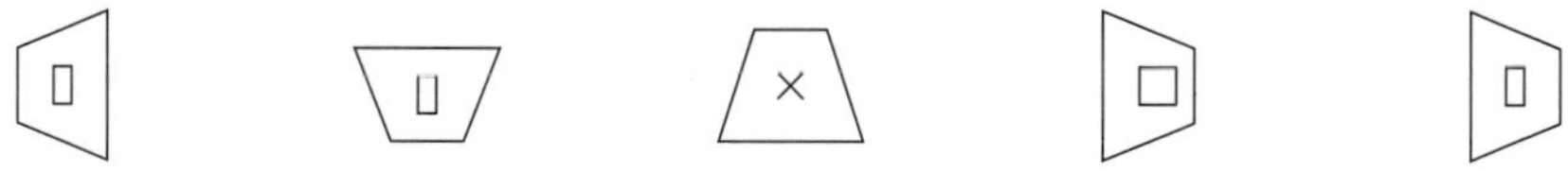
QE
QF
RG
SH

QG **a** QH **b**
RH **c** SE **d**
SF **e**

11

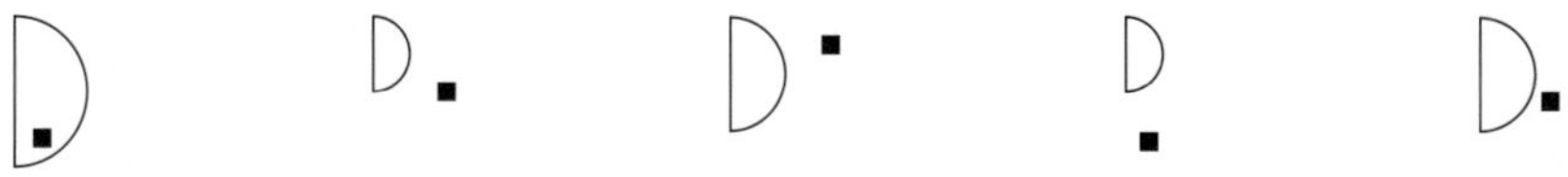
LA
MB
NC
LB

LC **a** MA **b**
MC **c** NA **d**
NB **e**

12

NS
OT
PT
PU

NT **a** NU **b**
OS **c** OU **d**
PS **e**

CONTINUE TO THE NEXT PAGE

Section 5

In the large square on the left one of the smaller squares is missing. Choose the shape or pattern that completes the square given.

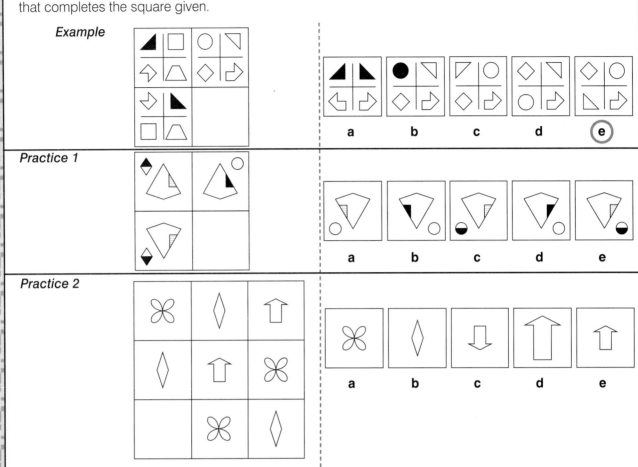

WAIT UNTIL YOU ARE TOLD TO GO ON

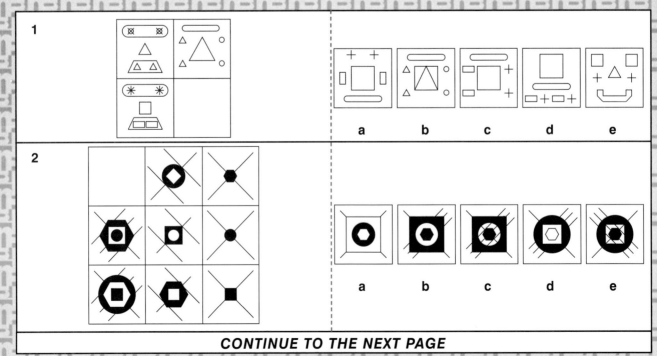

CONTINUE TO THE NEXT PAGE

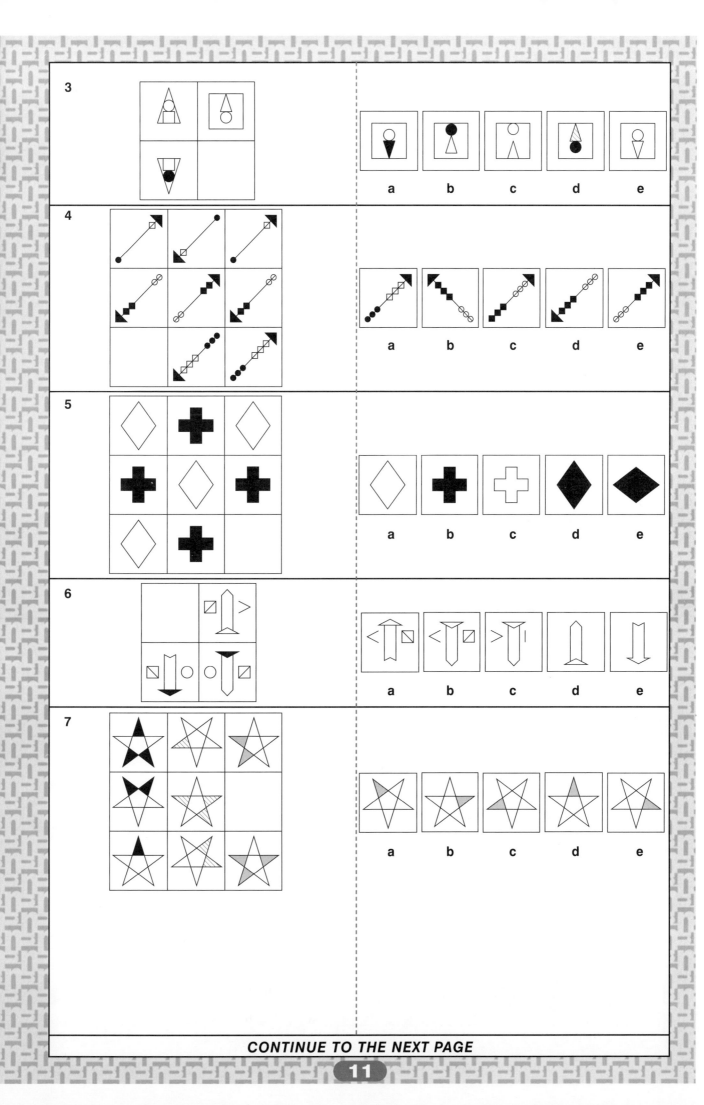

3

a b c d e

4

a b c d e

5

a b c d e

6

a b c d e

7

a b c d e

CONTINUE TO THE NEXT PAGE

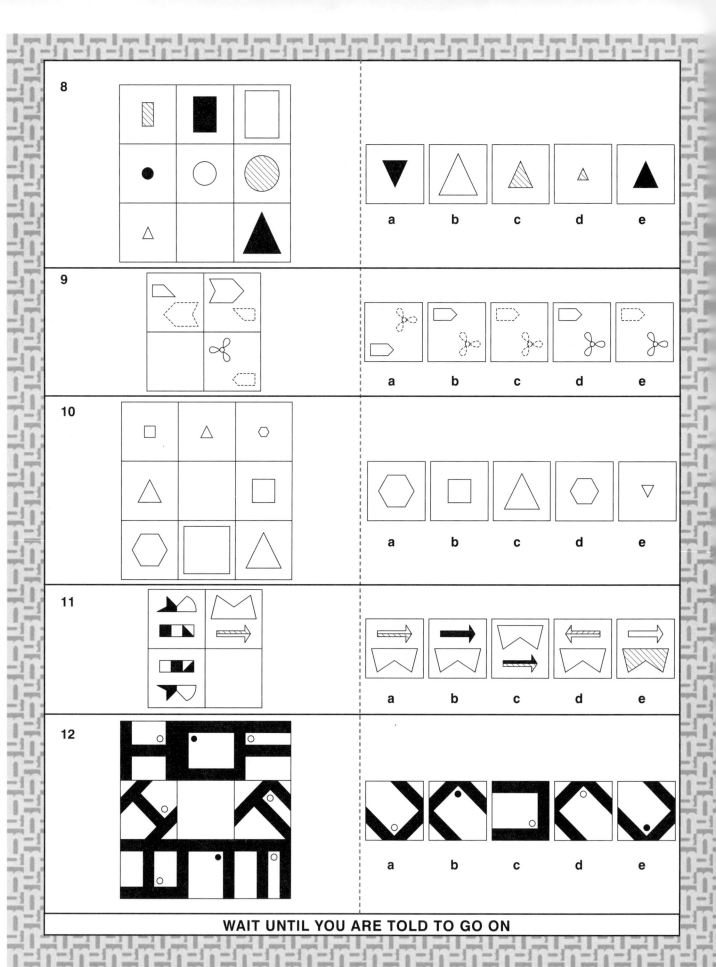

8

9

10

11

12

Bond 11+

Non-verbal Reasoning

Multiple-Choice Test 3

Read the following:

- Do not begin the test or open this booklet until told to do so.

- Work as quickly and as carefully as you can.

- Answers should be marked in the answer booklet provided, not in this test booklet.

- You may do rough working on a separate sheet of paper.

- If you make a mistake cross out the mistake and write the new answer clearly.

- Be careful to keep your place in the accompanying answer booklet.

- You will have 50 minutes to complete the test.

Text © Andrew Baines 2003

Original illustrations © Nelson Thornes Ltd 2003

The right of Andrew Baines to be identified as the author of this work has been asserted by him in acordance with the Copyright, Designs and Patents Act 1988.

Published in 2003 by:

Nelson Thornes Ltd, Delta Place, 27 Bath Road, CHELTENHAM, GL53 7TH, United Kingdom

01 02 03 04 05 / 10 9 8 7 6 5 4 3 2 1

A catalogue record for this book is available from the British Library

ISBN 0-7487-7329-0

Illustrations by Art Construction

Page make-up by AMR Ltd

Printed in Croatia by Zrinski

Nelson Thornes is a Wolters Kluwer company, and is not associated in any way with NFER-Nelson.

Section 1

Which pattern on the right completes the second pair in the same way as the first pair?

Example

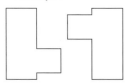 ?

a   b   c   (d)   e

Practice 1

   ?

a   b   c   d   e

Practice 2

   ?

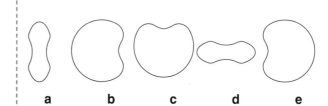

a   b   c   d   e

WAIT UNTIL YOU ARE TOLD TO GO ON

---

1    ?

      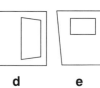

a   b   c   d   e

2  ?

a   b   c   d   e

3 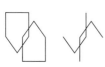 ?

a   b   c   d   e

CONTINUE TO THE NEXT PAGE

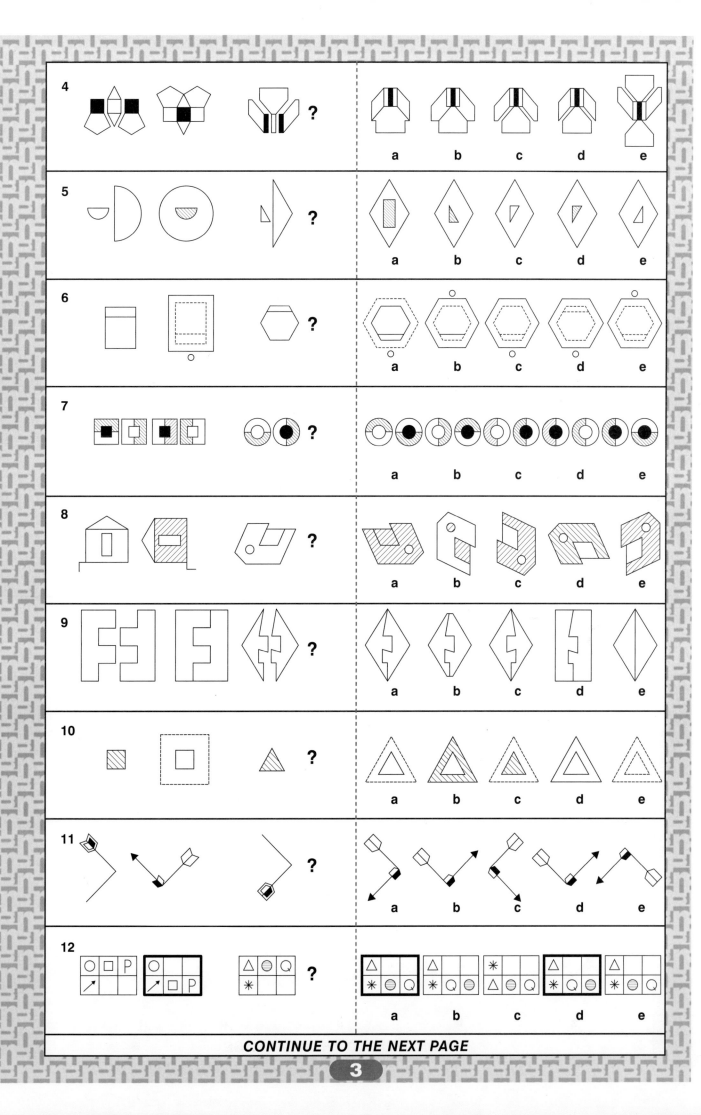

Section 2

Which pattern is the odd one out in each group?

Example

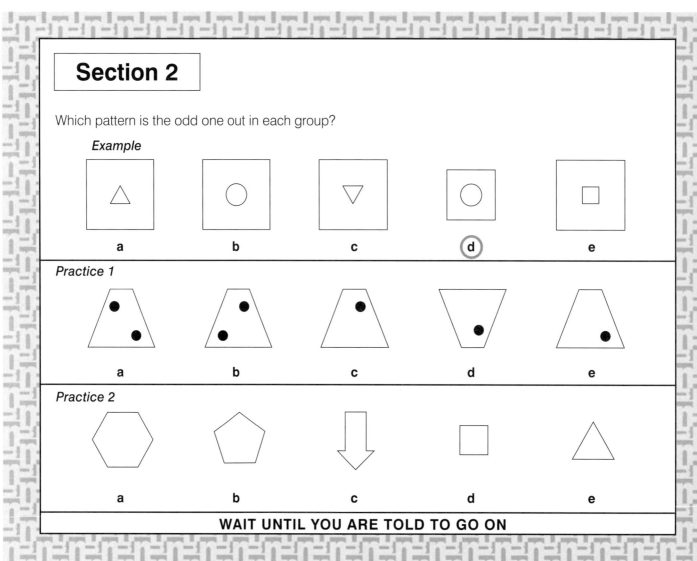

WAIT UNTIL YOU ARE TOLD TO GO ON

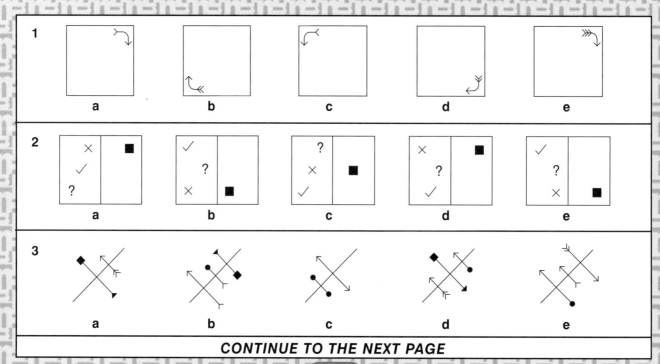

CONTINUE TO THE NEXT PAGE

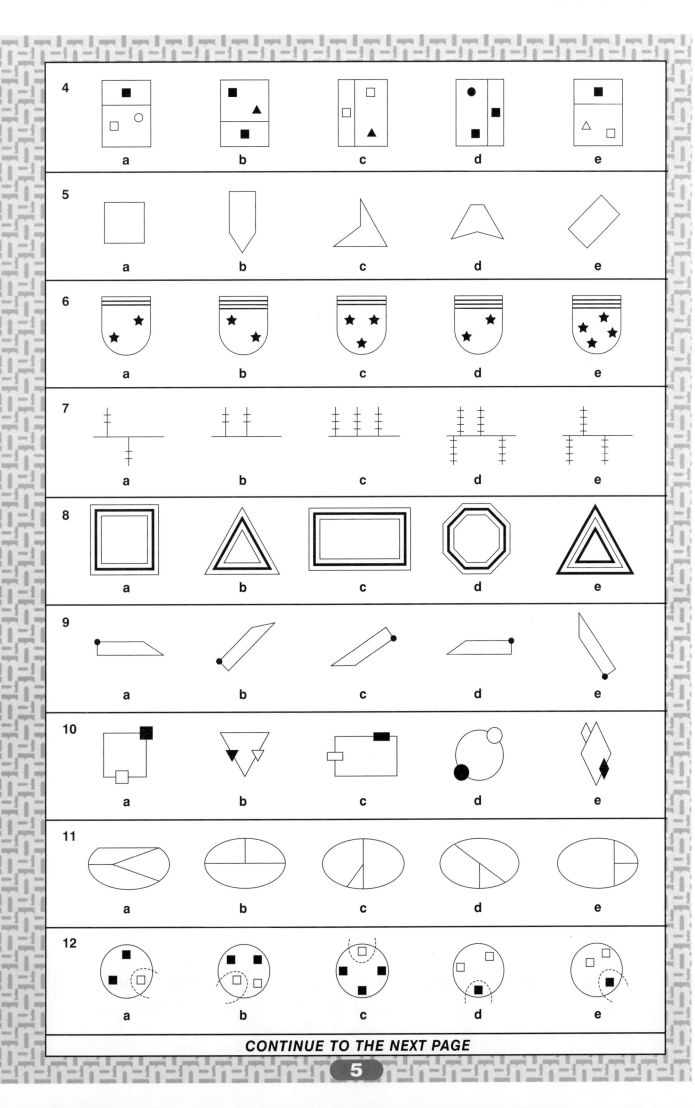

Section 3

The patterns below make a sequence. One pattern is missing. Which pattern completes the sequence?

Example

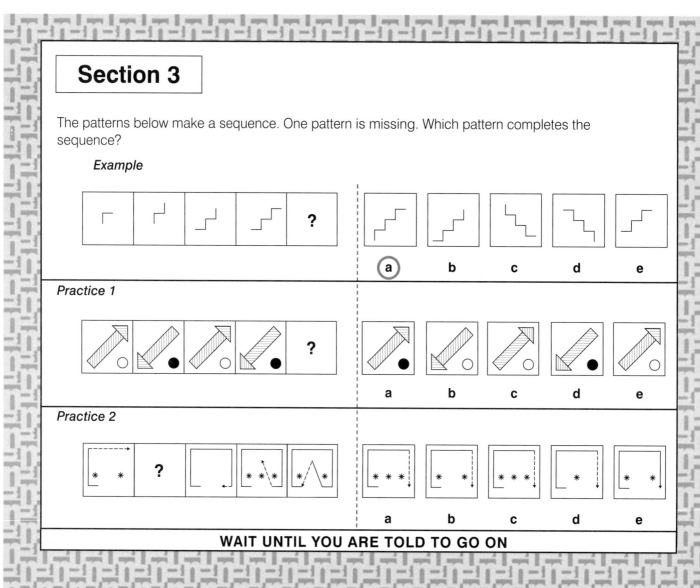

WAIT UNTIL YOU ARE TOLD TO GO ON

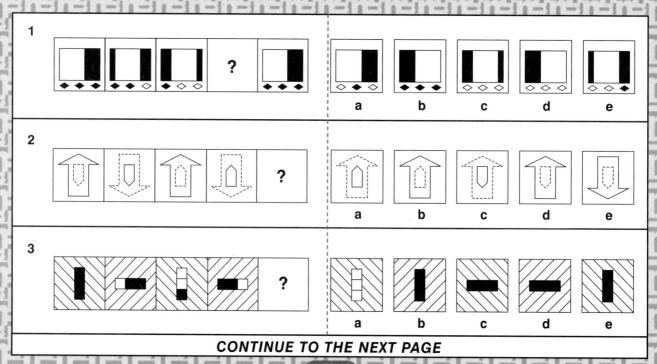

CONTINUE TO THE NEXT PAGE

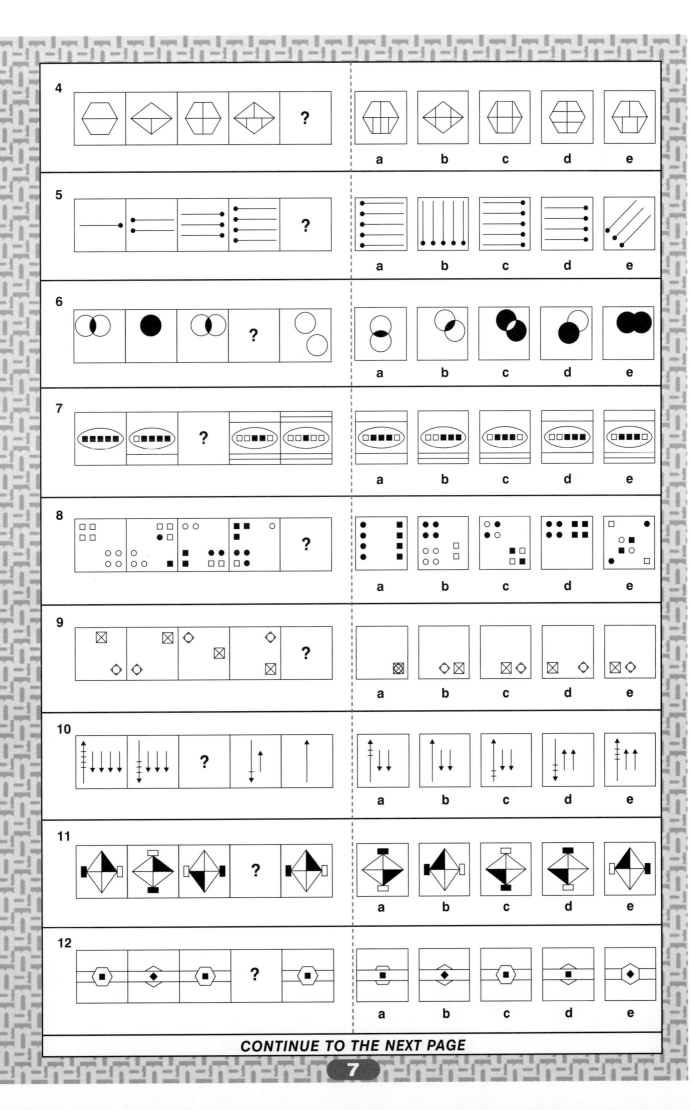

Section 4

Each of the patterns on the left has a two or three letter code. Select the correct code for the shape on the right following the same rules.

Example

EL

EM

FL

EM **a**	FM **(b)**
EL **c**	EF **d**
FL **e**	

Practice 1

RX

□
SX

⊙
RY

○

RY **a**	SX **b**
RS **c**	SY **d**
RX **e**	

Practice 2

PE

PF

⬡
QG

QE **a**	PF **b**
QF **c**	PE **d**
PG **e**	

WAIT UNTIL YOU ARE TOLD TO GO ON

1

JV

JW

KX

KV **a**	JX **b**
JW **c**	KW **d**
KX **e**	

2

FA

⬡
GB

⬡
HA

⬡

FB **a**	GA **b**
FA **c**	GB **d**
HB **e**	

3

RVE

SVF

TWF

RVF **a**	SVE **b**
TWE **c**	SWF **d**
TVE **e**	

CONTINUE TO THE NEXT PAGE

8

#							
4	EAJ	FAH	GBJ	FCH		EAH **a**	EBJ **b**
						FBJ **c**	GAB **d**
						GAH **e**	
5	RC	RD	SD	TE		RE **a**	SC **b**
						SE **c**	TD **d**
						TC **e**	
6	OHT	OIU	PHU	PIT		OHU **a**	OIT **b**
						PHT **c**	PIU **d**
						OHT **e**	
7	IRB	KRC	LSB	LSC		JRC **a**	JSB **b**
						JSK **c**	KSB **d**
						KSC **e**	
8	IV	JV	JW	KX		IW **a**	IX **b**
						JX **c**	KV **d**
						KW **e**	
9	HR	IS	IT			HS **a**	IS **b**
						HT **c**	HR **d**
						IR **e**	
10	DX	EX	FY	FZ		DY **a**	DZ **b**
						EY **c**	EZ **d**
						FX **e**	
11	MX	NY	MZ			NX **a**	NY **b**
						NZ **c**	MX **d**
						MY **e**	
12	FA	GB	FC			FB **a**	FA **b**
						GB **c**	GC **d**
						GA **e**	

CONTINUE TO THE NEXT PAGE

Section 5

In the large square on the left one of the smaller squares is missing. Choose the shape or pattern that completes the square given.

Example

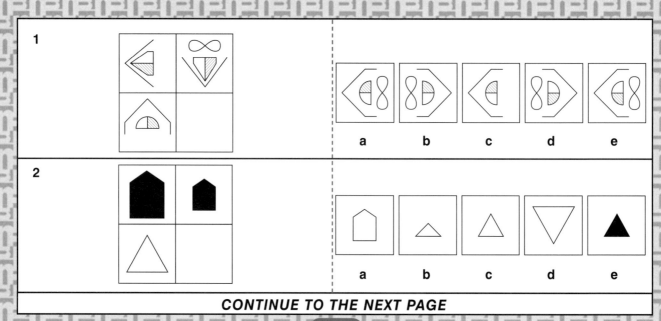

a	b	c	d	(e)

Practice 1

a	b	c	d	e

Practice 2

a	b	c	d	e

WAIT UNTIL YOU ARE TOLD TO GO ON

1

a	b	c	d	e

2

a	b	c	d	e

CONTINUE TO THE NEXT PAGE

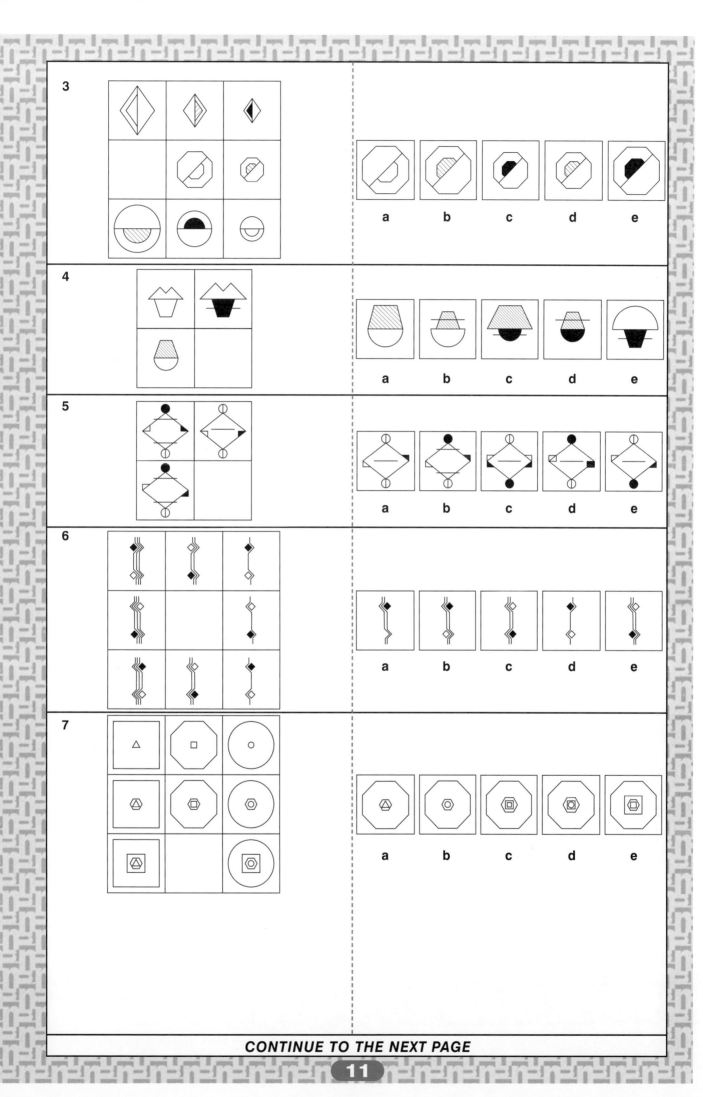

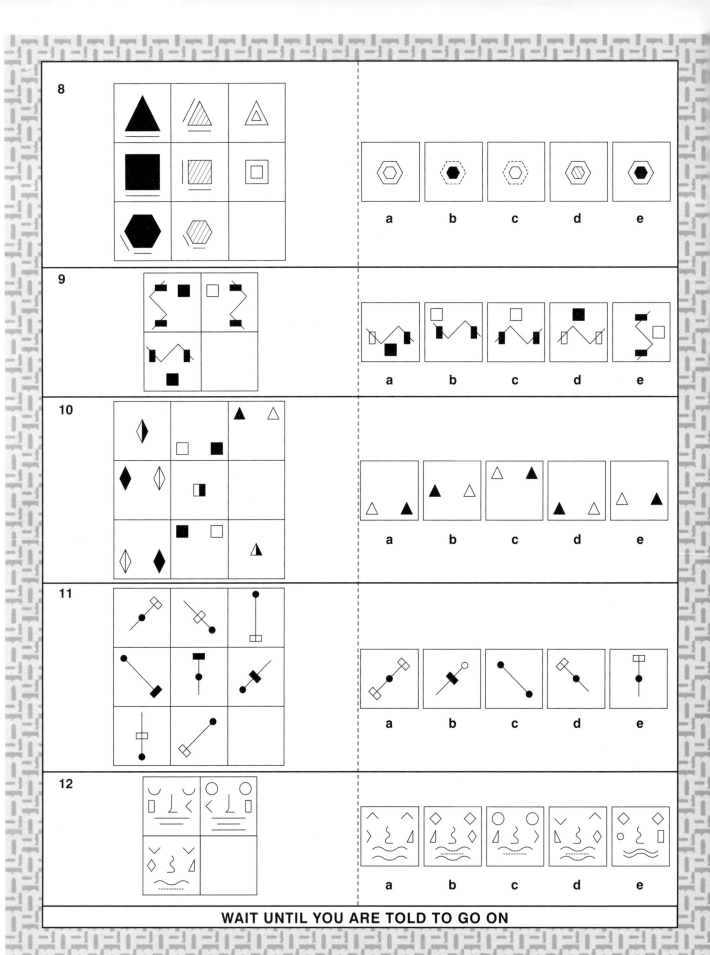

8

9

10

11

12

WAIT UNTIL YOU ARE TOLD TO GO ON

12

Bond 11+

Non-verbal Reasoning

Multiple-Choice Test 4

Read the following:

- Do not begin the test or open this booklet until told to do so.

- Work as quickly and as carefully as you can.

- Answers should be marked in the answer booklet provided, not in this test booklet.

- You may do rough working on a separate sheet of paper.

- If you make a mistake cross out the mistake and write the new answer clearly.

- Be careful to keep your place in the accompanying answer booklet.

- You will have 50 minutes to complete the test.

Text © Andrew Baines 2003

Original illustrations © Nelson Thornes Ltd 2003

The right of Andrew Baines to be identified as the author of this work has been asserted by him in acordance with the Copyright, Designs and Patents Act 1988.

All rights reserved, including translation. No part of this publication may be reproduced or transmitted in any form or by any means, electronic or mechanical, including photocopying, recording or duplication in any information storage and retrieval system, without permission in writing from the publisher or under licence from the Copyright Licensing Agency Ltd, of 90 Tottenham Court Road, London, W1T 4LP.

Any person who commits any unauthorised act in relation to this publication may be liable to criminal prosecution and civil claims for damages.

Published in 2003 by:

Nelson Thornes Ltd, Delta Place, 27 Bath Road, CHELTENHAM, GL53 7TH, United Kingdom

01 02 03 04 05 / 10 9 8 7 6 5 4 3 2 1

A catalogue record for this book is available from the British Library

ISBN 0-7487-7329-0

Illustrations by Art Construction

Page make-up by AMR Ltd

Printed in Croatia by Zrinski

Nelson Thornes is a Wolters Kluwer company, and is not associated in any way with NFER-Nelson.

Section 1

Which pattern on the right completes the second pair in the same way as the first pair?

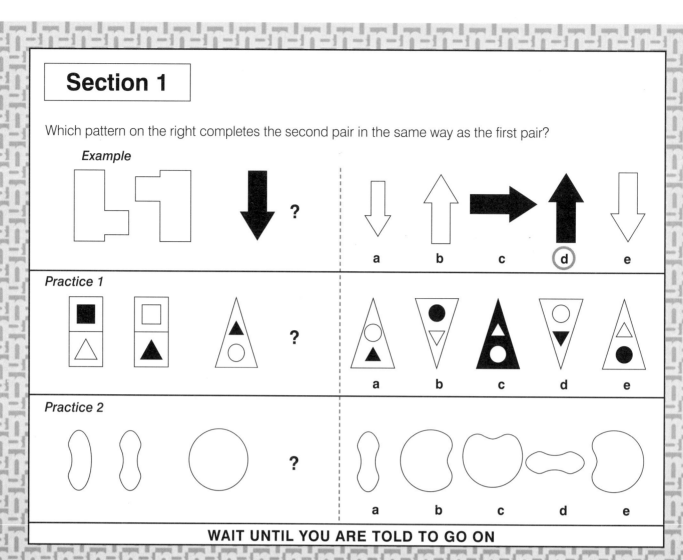

Example

a b c d e

Practice 1

a b c d e

Practice 2

a b c d e

WAIT UNTIL YOU ARE TOLD TO GO ON

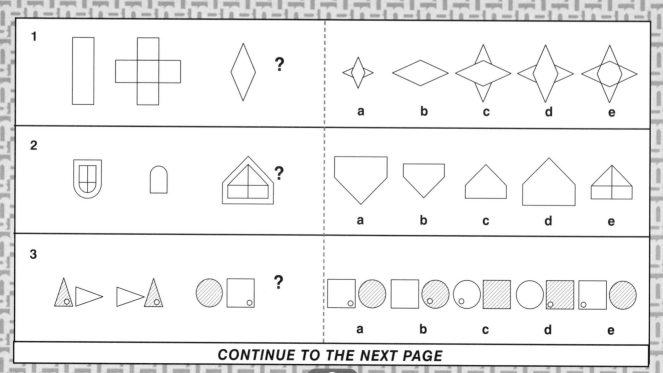

1

a b c d e

2

a b c d e

3

a b c d e

CONTINUE TO THE NEXT PAGE

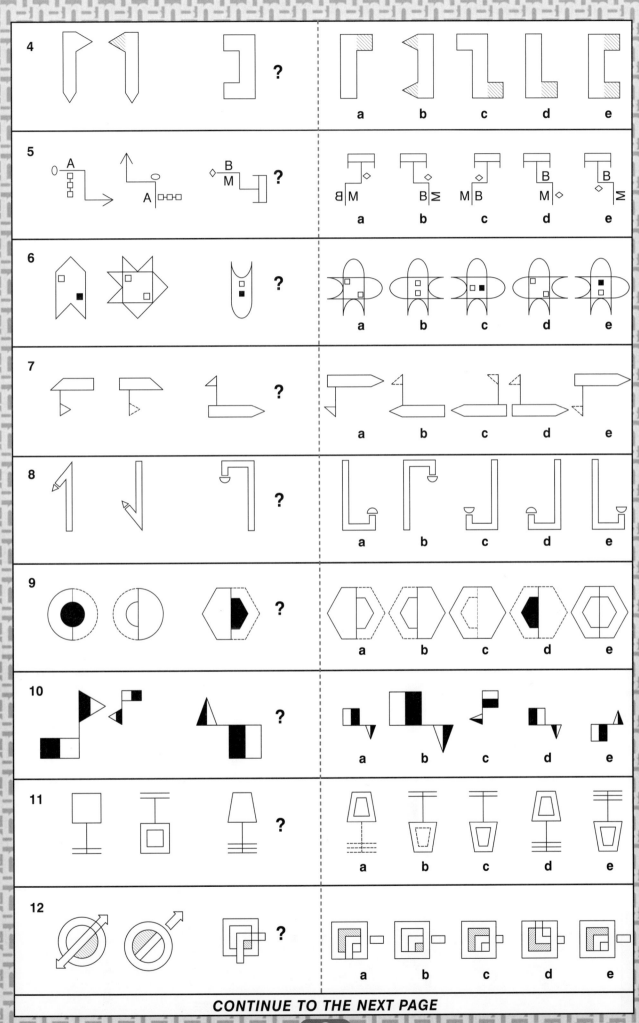

Section 2

Which pattern is the odd one out in each group?

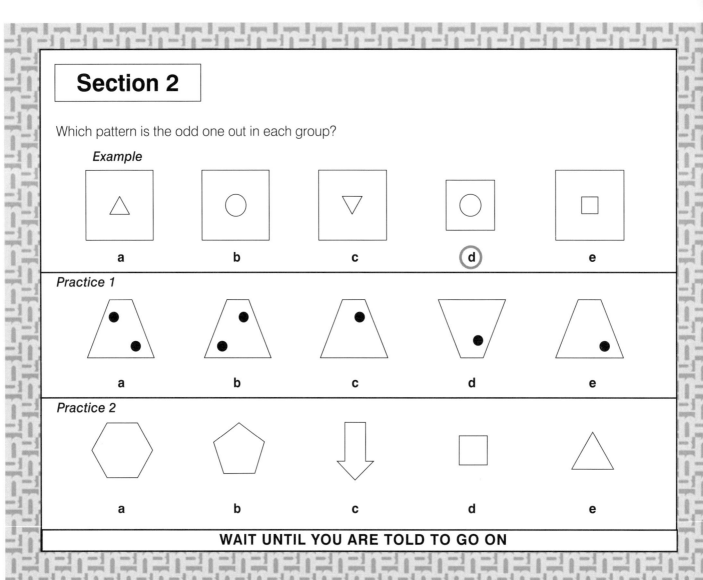

Example

a   b   c   d   e

Practice 1

a   b   c   d   e

Practice 2

a   b   c   d   e

WAIT UNTIL YOU ARE TOLD TO GO ON

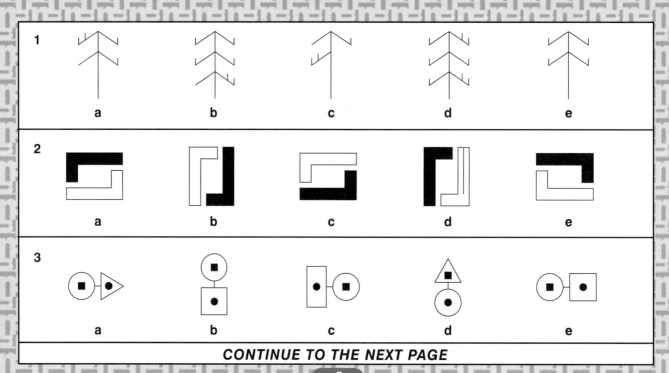

1   a   b   c   d   e

2   a   b   c   d   e

3   a   b   c   d   e

CONTINUE TO THE NEXT PAGE

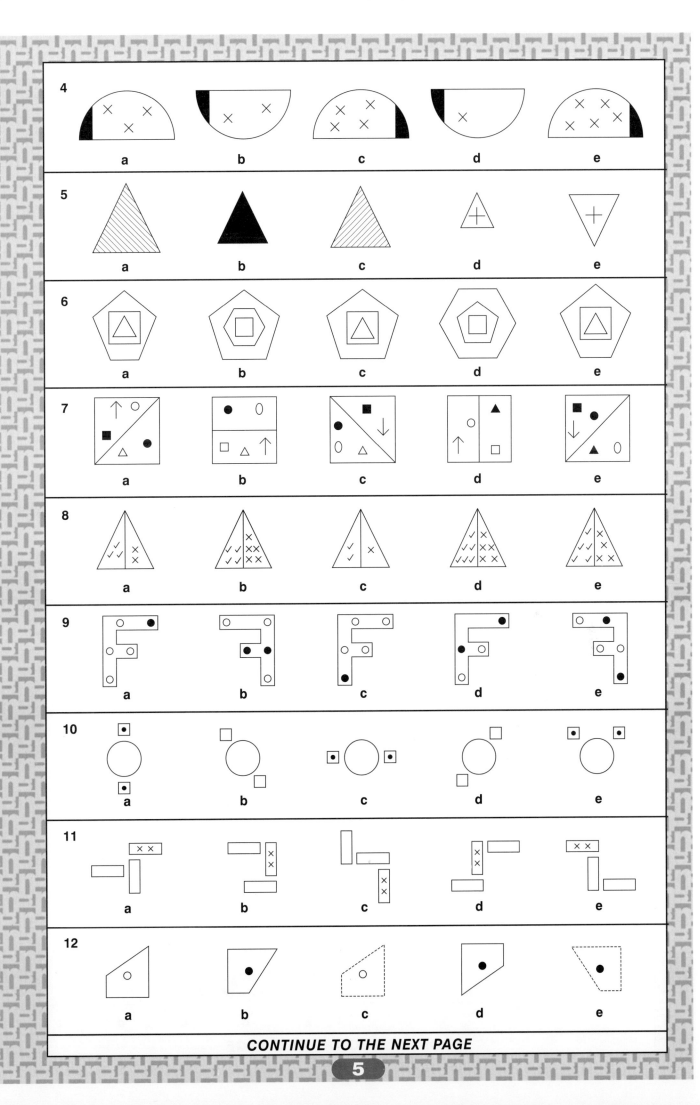

Section 3

The patterns below make a sequence. One pattern is missing. Which pattern completes the sequence?

Example

				?

a b c d e

Practice 1

a b c d e

Practice 2

a b c d e

WAIT UNTIL YOU ARE TOLD TO GO ON

1

a b c d e

2

a b c d e

3

a b c d e

CONTINUE TO THE NEXT PAGE

6

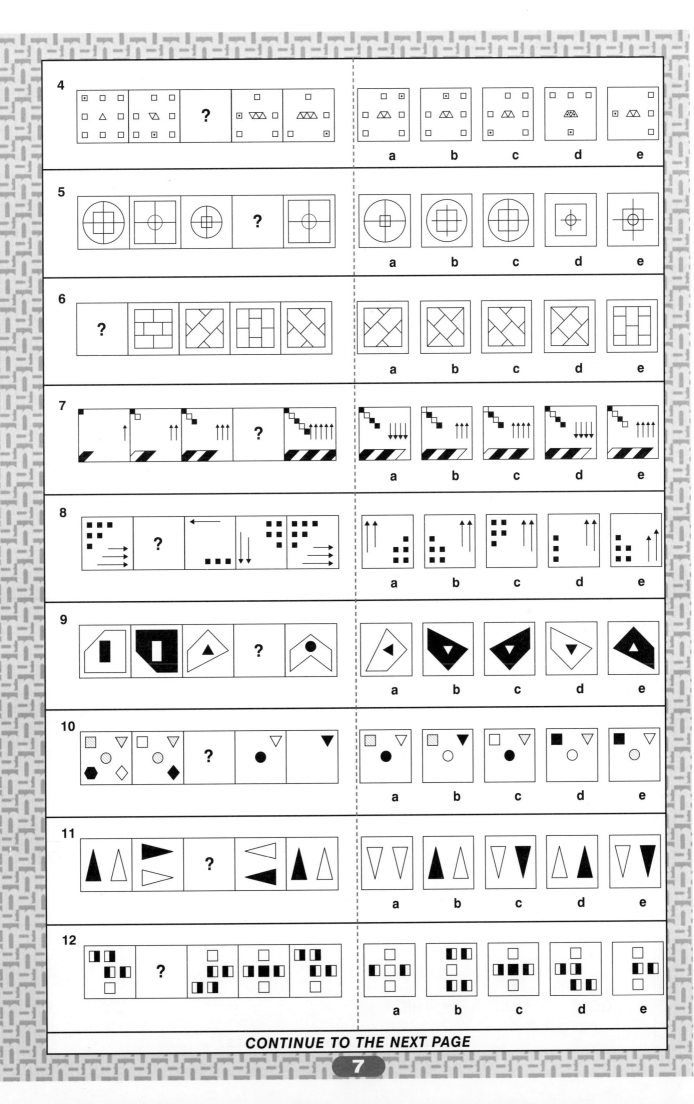

Section 4

Each of the patterns on the left has a two or three letter code. Select the correct code for the shape on the right following the same rules.

Example

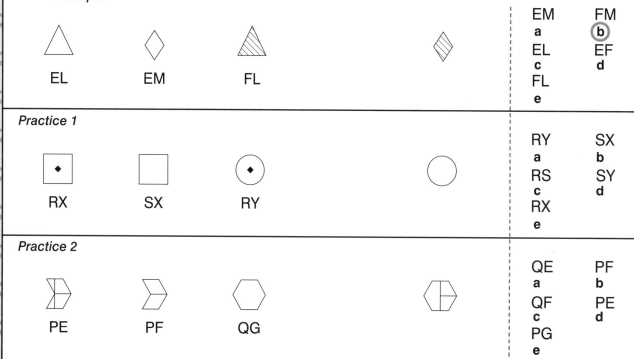

EM **a**	FM **(b)**
EL **c**	EF **d**
FL **e**	

EL   EM   FL

Practice 1

RY **a**	SX **b**
RS **c**	SY **d**
RX **e**	

RX   SX   RY

Practice 2

QE **a**	PF **b**
QF **c**	PE **d**
PG **e**	

PE   PF   QG

WAIT UNTIL YOU ARE TOLD TO GO ON

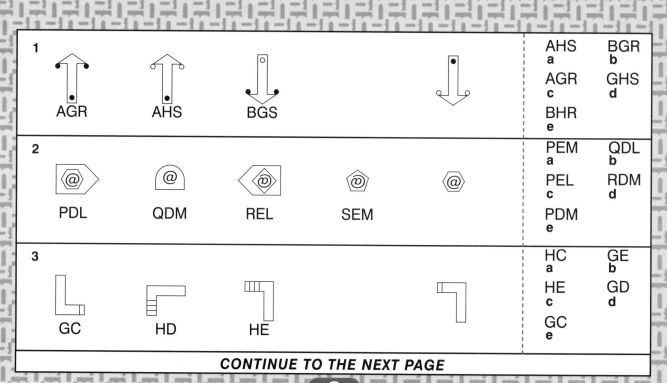

1

AHS **a**	BGR **b**
AGR **c**	GHS **d**
BHR **e**	

AGR   AHS   BGS

2

PEM **a**	QDL **b**
PEL **c**	RDM **d**
PDM **e**	

PDL   QDM   REL   SEM

3

HC **a**	GE **b**
HE **c**	GD **d**
GC **e**	

GC   HD   HE

CONTINUE TO THE NEXT PAGE

8

#	Symbols					Answer options	
4	VFA	VGB	WGC	XHC		a VHC / c WGB / e XHA	b WFA / d XFB
5	NI	OI	PJ			a OI / c NJ / e PJ	b NI / d OJ
6	AW	BX	CX			a AX / c BW / e CW	b BX / d AW
7	LC	MD	ND			a MD / c LD / e NC	b LC / d MC
8	LX	MY	MZ	NY		a LY / c MX / e NZ	b LZ / d NX
9	MA	MB	NC	OC		a MC / c NB / e OB	b NA / d OA
10	FP	FQ	GR			a GR / c GP / e FQ	b FR / d GQ
11	YAF	YAG	XBG			a XAG / c YAF / e YBG	b XBF / d YBF
12	MFR	MGS	NFS			a MFS / c NFR / e NGS	b MGR / d NGR

CONTINUE TO THE NEXT PAGE

Section 5

In the large square on the left one of the smaller squares is missing. Choose the shape or pattern that completes the square given.

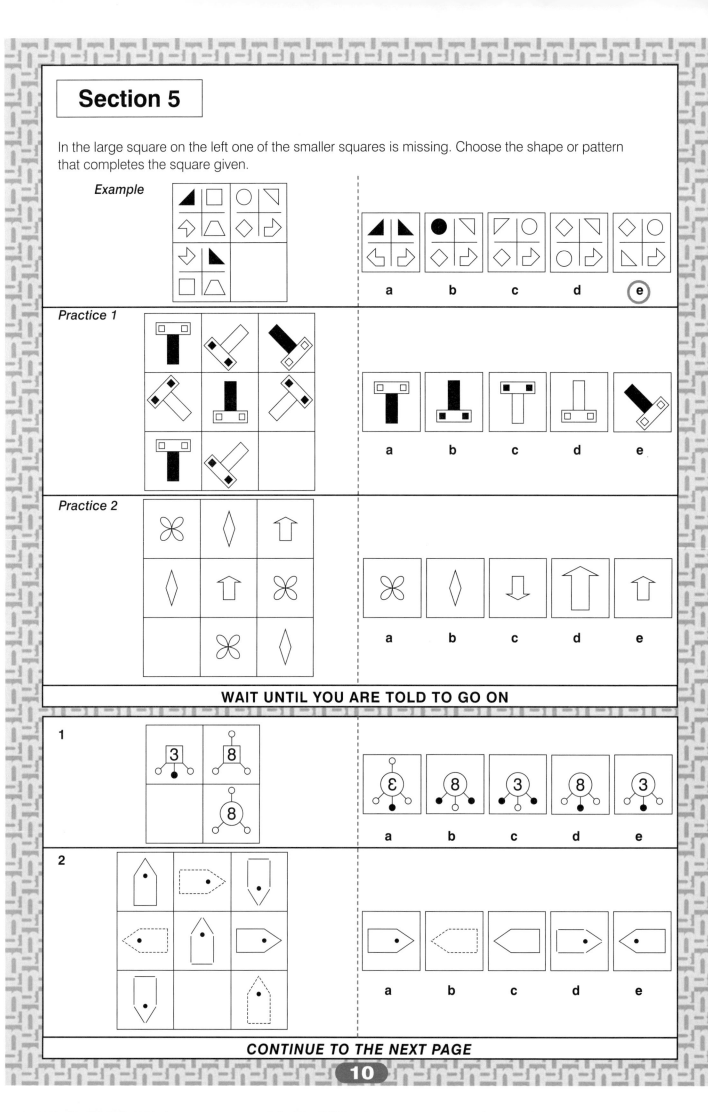

Example

a   b   c   d   (e)

Practice 1

a   b   c   d   e

Practice 2

a   b   c   d   e

WAIT UNTIL YOU ARE TOLD TO GO ON

1

a   b   c   d   e

2

a   b   c   d   e

CONTINUE TO THE NEXT PAGE

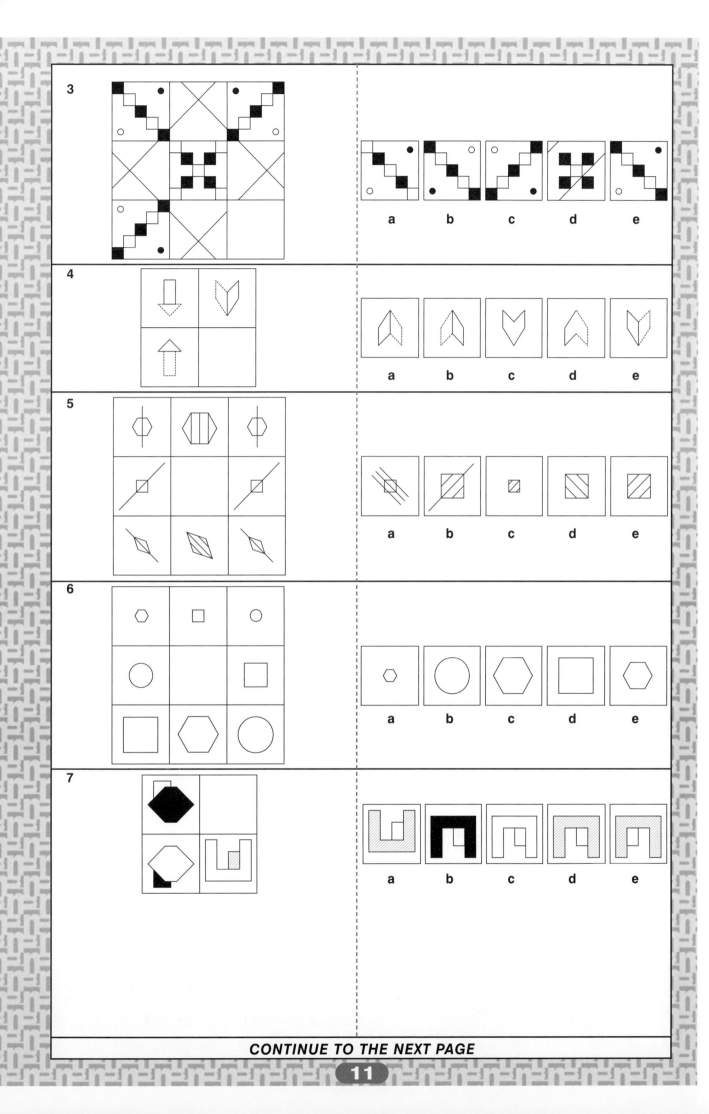

3

a b c d e

4

a b c d e

5

a b c d e

6

a b c d e

7

a b c d e

CONTINUE TO THE NEXT PAGE

11

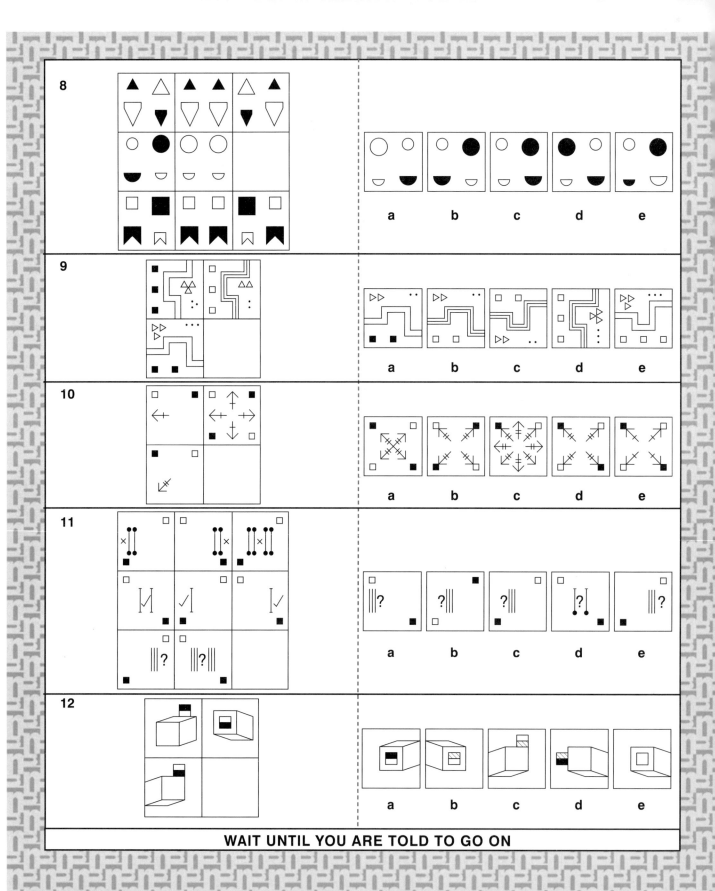

WAIT UNTIL YOU ARE TOLD TO GO ON

Bond 11+

TEST PAPERS

Answer sheets for Multiple Choice Tests

All of the answer sheets for Bond 11+ Test Papers Multiple-Choice versions are included in this booklet. Please ensure you are using the correct answer sheet for the test you are taking. The tests covered in this booklet are Maths 1–4, Non-verbal Reasoning 1–4 and Verbal Reasoning 1–4.

Text © Andrew Baines 2003

The right of Andrew Baines to be identified as author of this work has been asserted by him in accordance with the Copyright, Designs and Patents Act 1988.

All rights reserved. No part of this publication may be reproduced or transmitted in any form or by any means, electronic or mechanical, including photocopy, recording or any information storage and retrieval system, without permission in writing from the publisher or under licence from the Copyright Licensing Agency Limited, of 90 Tottenham Court Road, London W1T 4LP.

Any person who commits any unauthorised act in relation to this publication may be liable to criminal prosecution and civil claims for damages.

Published in 2003 by:
Nelson Thornes Ltd
Delta Place
27 Bath Road
CHELTENHAM
GL53 7TH
United Kingdom

03 04 05 06 07 / 10 9 8 7 6 5 4 3 2 1

A catalogue record for this book is available from the British Library

ISBN 0-7487-7329-0

Page make-up by IFA Design Ltd, Plymouth, Devon

Printed and bound in Croatia by Zrinski

Published by Nelson Thornes. Nelson Thornes is a Wolters Kluwer company, and is not associated in any way with NFER-Nelson.

Bond 11+ Maths Test 1

Name

1 D E F G H

2 A B C D E

3 A B C D E

4 A B C D E

5 A B C D E

6 P Q R S T

7 A B C D E

8 A B C D E

9 A B C D E

10 A B C D E

11 A B C D E

12 A B C D E

13 A B C D E

14 A B C D E

15 A B C D E

16 A B C D E

17 A B C D E

18 A B C D E

19 A B C D E

20 A B C D E

21 A B C D E

22 A B C D E

23 A B C D E

24 A B C D E

25 A B C D E

26 A B C D E

27 A B C D E

28 A B C D E

29 A B C D E

30 A B C D E

31 A B C D E

32 A B C D E

33 A B C D E

34 A B C D E

35 A B C D E

36 A B C D E

37 A B C D E

38 A B C D E

39 A B C D E

40 A B C D E

41 A B C D E

42 A B C D E

43 A B C D E

44 A B C D E

45 A B C D E

46 A B C D E

47 A B C D E

48 A B C D E

49 A B C D E

50 A B C D E

Bond 11+ Maths Test 2

Name

1
A
B
C
D
E

2
A
B
C
D
E

3
A
B
C
D
E

4
A
B
C
D
E

5
A
B
C
D
E

6
A
B
C
D
E

7
A
B
C
D
E

8
A
B
C
D
E

9
A
B
C
D
E

10
A
B
C
D
E

11
A
B
C
D
E

12
A
B
C
D
E

13
A
B
C
D
E

14
A
B
C
D
E

15
A
B
C
D
E

16
A
B
C
D
E

17
A
B
C
D
E

18
A
B
C
D
E

19
A
B
C
D
E

20
A
B
C
D
E

21
A
B
C
D
E

22
A
B
C
D
E

23
A
B
C
D
E

24
A
B
C
D
E

25
A
B
C
D
E

26
A
B
C
D
E

27
A
B
C
D
E

28
A
B
C
D
E

29
A
B
C
D
E

30
A
B
C
D
E

31
A
B
C
D
E

32
A
B
C
D
E

33
A
B
C
D
E

34
A
B
C
D
E

35
A
B
C
D
E

36
A
B
C
D
E

37
A
B
C
D
E

38
A
B
C
D
E

39
A
B
C
D
E

40
A
B
C
D
E

41
A
B
C
D
E

42
A
B
C
D
E

43
A
B
C
D
E

44
A
B
C
D
E

45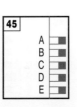
A
B
C
D
E

46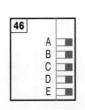
A
B
C
D
E

47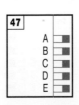
A
B
C
D
E

48
A
B
C
D
E

49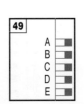
A
B
C
D
E

50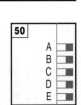
A
B
C
D
E

Bond 11+ Maths Test 3

Name

1	A B C D E
2	A B C D E
3	A B C D E
4	A B C D E
5	A B C D E
6	A B C D E
7	A B C D E

8	A B C D E
9	A B C D E
10	A B C D E
11	A B C D E
12	A B C D E
13	A B C D E
14	A B C D E

15	A B C D E
16	A B C D E
17	A B C D E
18	A B C D E
19	COX NON DAD MUM HIT
20	A B C D E
21	A B C D E

22	A B C D E
23	A B C D E
24	A B C D E
25	A B C D E
26	A B C D E
27	A B C D E
28	A B C D E

29	A B C D E
30	A B C D E
31	A B C D E
32	A B C D E
33	A B C D E
34	A B C D E
35	A B C D E

36	A B C D E
37	A B C D E
38	A B C D E
39	A B C D E
40	A B C D E
41	A B C D E
42	A B C D E

43	A B C D E
44	R S T U V
45	A B C D E
46	A B C D E
47	A B C D E
48	A B C D E
49	A B C D E
50	A B C D E

Bond 11+ Maths Test 4

Name

1 A B C D E

2 A B C D E

3 A B C D E

4 A B C D E

5 A B C D E

6 A B C D E

7 A B C D E

8 A B C D E

9 A B C D E

10 A B C D E

11 A B C D E

12 A B C D E

13 A B C D E

14 A B C D E

15 A B C D E

16 A B C D E

17 A B C D E

18 A B C D E

19 A B C D E

20 A B C D E

21 A B C D E

22 A B C D E

23 A B C D E

24 A B C D E

25 A B C D E

26 A B C D E

27 A B C D E

28 NOZE NOS HOSE ICON TON

29 A B C D E

30 A B C D E

31 A B C D E

32 A B C D E

33 A B C D E

34 A B C D E

35 A B C D E

36 A B C D E

37 A B C D E

38 A B C D E

39 A B C D E

40 A B C D E

41 A B C D E

42 A B C D E

43 A B C D E

44 A B C D E

45 A B C D E

46 A B C D E

47 A B C D E

48 A B C D E

49 A B C D E

50 A B C D E

Bond 11+ Non-verbal Reasoning Test 1

Name

Section 1

Practice 1	Practice 2	1	2	3	4	5	6
a b c d e	a b c d e	a b c d e	a b c d e	a b c d e	a b c d e	a b c d e	a b c d e

Section 2

7	8	9	10	11	12	Practice 1	Practice 2
a b c d e	a b c d e	a b c d e	a b c d e	a b c d e	a b c d e	a b c d e	a b c d e

1	2	3	4	5	6	7	8	9
a b c d e	a b c d e	a b c d e	a b c d e	a b c d e	a b c d e	a b c d e	a b c d e	a b c d e

Section 3

10	11	12	Practice 1	Practice 2	1	2	3	4
a b c d e	a b c d e	a b c d e	a b c d e	a b c d e	a b c d e	a b c d e	a b c d e	a b c d e

Section 4

5	6	7	8	9	10	11	12	Practice 1
a b c d e	a b c d e	a b c d e	a b c d e	a b c d e	a b c d e	a b c d e	a b c d e	a b c d e

Practice 2	1	2	3	4	5	6	7	8
a b c d e	a b c d e	a b c d e	a b c d e	a b c d e	a b c d e	a b c d e	a b c d e	a b c d e

Section 5

9	10	11	12	Practice 1	Practice 2	1	2	3
a b c d e	a b c d e	a b c d e	a b c d e	a b c d e	a b c d e	a b c d e	a b c d e	a b c d e

4	5	6	7	8	9	10	11	12
a b c d e	a b c d e	a b c d e	a b c d e	a b c d e	a b c d e	a b c d e	a b c d e	a b c d e

Bond 11+ Non-verbal Reasoning Test 2

Name

Section 1

| Practice 1 | Practice 2 | 1 | 2 | 3 | 4 | 5 | 6 |

a b c d e (for each)

| 7 | 8 | 9 | 10 | 11 | 12 |

Section 2

| Practice 1 | Practice 2 |

| 1 | 2 | 3 | 4 | 5 | 6 | 7 | 8 | 9 |

| 10 | 11 | 12 |

Section 3

| Practice 1 | Practice 2 | 1 | 2 | 3 | 4 |

| 5 | 6 | 7 | 8 | 9 | 10 | 11 | 12 |

Section 4

| Practice 1 |

| Practice 2 | 1 | 2 | 3 | 4 | 5 | 6 | 7 | 8 |

| 9 | 10 | 11 | 12 |

Section 5

| Practice 1 | Practice 2 | 1 | 2 | 3 |

| 4 | 5 | 6 | 7 | 8 | 9 | 10 | 11 | 12 |

Bond 11+ Non-verbal Reasoning Test 3

Name

Section 1

Practice 1	Practice 2	1	2	3	4	5	6
a b c d e	a b c d e	a b c d e	a b c d e	a b c d e	a b c d e	a b c d e	a b c d e

7	8	9	10	11	12	**Section 2** Practice 1	Practice 2
a b c d e	a b c d e	a b c d e	a b c d e	a b c d e	a b c d e	a b c d e	a b c d e

1	2	3	4	5	6	7	8	9
a b c d e	a b c d e	a b c d e	a b c d e	a b c d e	a b c d e	a b c d e	a b c d e	a b c d e

Section 3

10	11	12	Practice 1	Practice 2	1	2	3	4
a b c d e	a b c d e	a b c d e	a b c d e	a b c d e	a b c d e	a b c d e	a b c d e	a b c d e

5	6	7	8	9	10	11	12	**Section 4** Practice 1
a b c d e	a b c d e	a b c d e	a b c d e	a b c d e	a b c d e	a b c d e	a b c d e	a b c d e

Practice 2	1	2	3	4	5	6	7	8
a b c d e	a b c d e	a b c d e	a b c d e	a b c d e	a b c d e	a b c d e	a b c d e	a b c d e

Section 5

9	10	11	12	Practice 1	Practice 2	1	2	3
a b c d e	a b c d e	a b c d e	a b c d e	a b c d e	a b c d e	a b c d e	a b c d e	a b c d e

4	5	6	7	8	9	10	11	12
a b c d e	a b c d e	a b c d e	a b c d e	a b c d e	a b c d e	a b c d e	a b c d e	a b c d e

Bond 11+ Non-verbal Reasoning Test 4

Name

Section 1

Practice 1	Practice 2	1	2	3	4	5	6
a b c d e	a b c d e	a b c d e	a b c d e	a b c d e	a b c d e	a b c d e	a b c d e

Section 2

7	8	9	10	11	12	Practice 1	Practice 2
a b c d e	a b c d e	a b c d e	a b c d e	a b c d e	a b c d e	a b c d e	a b c d e

1	2	3	4	5	6	7	8	9
a b c d e	a b c d e	a b c d e	a b c d e	a b c d e	a b c d e	a b c d e	a b c d e	a b c d e

Section 3

10	11	12	Practice 1	Practice 2	1	2	3	4
a b c d e	a b c d e	a b c d e	a b c d e	a b c d e	a b c d e	a b c d e	a b c d e	a b c d e

Section 4

5	6	7	8	9	10	11	12	Practice 1
a b c d e	a b c d e	a b c d e	a b c d e	a b c d e	a b c d e	a b c d e	a b c d e	a b c d e

Practice 2	1	2	3	4	5	6	7	8
a b c d e	a b c d e	a b c d e	a b c d e	a b c d e	a b c d e	a b c d e	a b c d e	a b c d e

Section 5

9	10	11	12	Practice 1	Practice 2	1	2	3
a b c d e	a b c d e	a b c d e	a b c d e	a b c d e	a b c d e	a b c d e	a b c d e	a b c d e

4	5	6	7	8	9	10	11	12
a b c d e	a b c d e	a b c d e	a b c d e	a b c d e	a b c d e	a b c d e	a b c d e	a b c d e

Name

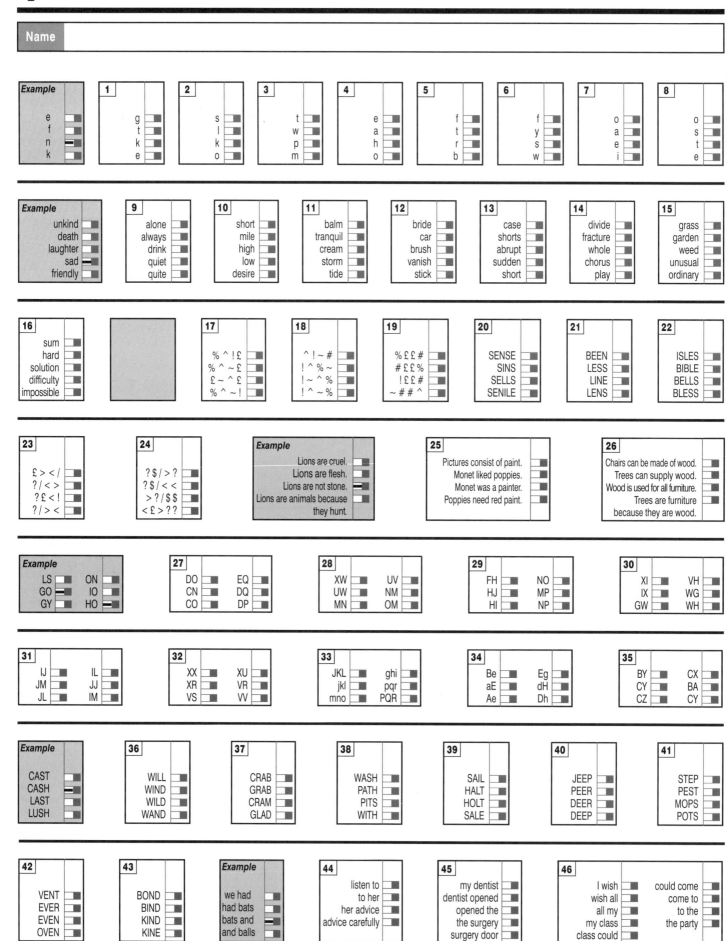

47

come to	□	to the	□
the back	□	back door	□
door of	□	of the	□
the new	□	new building	□

48

the squid	□	squid stretched	□
stretched a	□	a tentacle	□
tentacle over	□	over yellow	□
yellow weed	□		

49

take your	□	your litter	□
litter home	□	home never	□
never drop	□	drop it	□

50

the weather	□	weather forecast	□
forecast for	□	for this	□
this evening	□	evening is	□
is appalling	□		

51

the kite	□	kite string	□
string was	□	was caught	□
caught in	□	in the	□
the tree	□		

52

Paul	□	Judy	□
Peter	□	Beth	□
Toby	□	Suzy	□
Jon	□	Emily	□
Sue	□	Gary	□

53

Paul	□	Judy	□
Peter	□	Beth	□
Toby	□	Suzy	□
Jon	□	Emily	□
Sue	□	Gary	□

54

Paul	□	Judy	□
Peter	□	Beth	□
Toby	□	Suzy	□
Jon	□	Emily	□
Sue	□	Gary	□

Example

hand	□	light	□
green	▭	house	▭
for	□	sure	□

55

sun	□	shone	□
cloud	□	fall	□
rain	□	pour	□

56

moth	□	hop	□
ant	□	eater	□
frig	□	tick	□

57

act	□	role	□
play	□	cast	□
sausage	□	room	□

58

at	□	side	□
by	□	wide	□
in	□	last	□

59

hind	□	sight	□
right	□	deer	□
rain	□	fell	□

60

for	□	gear	□
four	□	place	□
fore	□	leg	□

61

up	□	left	□
under	□	right	□
stand	□	sit	□

62

to	□	age	□
by	□	way	□
in	□	held	□

Example

shunt	□	hip	□
hot	▭	ship	□
shut	□	snip	▭

63

duo	□	singe	□
due	□	sting	□
doe	□	stung	□

64

right	□	meter	□
fight	□	frame	□
tight	□	timer	□

65

read	□	rota	□
bead	□	riot	□
bred	□	brat	□

66

limb	□	stalk	□
slim	□	crack	□
clam	□	break	□

67

slay	□	rumble	□
spay	□	crumbs	□
play	□	crumple	□

68

lease	□	pills	□
pease	□	spill	□
place	□	still	□

69

rain	□	apple	□
tray	□	pleat	□
tail	□	treat	□

70

slit	□	pint	□
spit	□	sign	□
pile	□	spin	□

71

horse	□	burns	□
hoses	□	sunny	□
roses	□	basin	□

Example

tree	□	thin	□
short	▭	white	□
colour	□	wide	▭

72

colour	□	paint	□
crimson	□	cloud	□
danger	□	azure	□

73

impolite	□	unpleasant	□
rude	□	nasty	□
manners	□	sunny	□

74

hour	□	clock	□
tiny	□	time	□
second	□	huge	□

75

paint	□	artist	□
painter	□	page	□
brush	□	author	□

76

collar	□	saddle	□
paw	□	hoof	□
bark	□	stable	□

77

six	□	web	□
insect	□	eight	□
ladybird	□	spin	□

78

bedroom	□	football	□
sheet	□	chess	□
sleep	□	play	□

79

sty	□	milk	□
pork	□	moo	□
mud	□	cowshed	□

80

mountain	□	flower	□
ascend	□	age	□
descend	□	shrink	□

Name

Example
we had
had bats
bats and
and balls

1
pigs eat
eat different
different sorts
sorts of
of scraps

2
please do / do not
not leave / leave in
in such / such a
a rush

3
Jack's solo / solo was
was in / in the
the final / final song

4
it would / would be
be better / better to
to go / go another
another evening

5
Sarah's car / car would
would not / not start
start this / this morning

6
climbing a / a mountain
mountain is / is a challenge
challenge for / for most
most people

7
biscuits often / often contain
contain high / high levels
levels of / of sugar

8
Amy immediately / immediately posted
posted her / her cards
cards as / as she
she addressed / addressed them

9
south
north
south east
south west

10
north west
south west
east
south

11
north west
north east
south
south west

12
1234
1243
1432
6234

13
6241
4621
6421
6124

14
STAR
YARD
DEAR
READ

15
DART
TRAY
STAR
ARTS

16
9345
5493
9348
5293

17
9345
5493
9348
5293

18
9345
5493
9348
5293

19
9345
5493
9348
5293

Example
stone
tyres
ration
nation
noisy

20
shard
dusty
thuds
rusty
hurry

21
staring
string
laser
grass
strain

22
nasty
stern
banter
rinse
tribe

23
house
honest
teeth
heels
those

24
swear
drawer
snared
swede
waned

25
fared
leader
flared
deaf
ladder

26
flower
fault
crow
frolic
crawl

27
fling
valour
gravel
grain
flour

28
drain
darts
dines
snare
nested

29
p
q
r
s
t

30
p
q
r
s
t

31
p
q
r
s
t

32
p
q
r
s
t

33
p
q
r
s
t

34
p
q
r
s
t

35
p
q
r
s
t

36
p
q
r
s
t

Example
price
hasten
strike
charge
money

37
weapon
spade
jewel
garden
heart

38
wedding
ring
line
valuable
rich

39
pile
fence
cheque
ditch
bank

40
stable
ride
house
reliable
sound

41
fraction
fork
cutlery
cut
food

42
fortify
key
bolt
escape
hide

43
suit
bond
chest
neck
tie

44
pursue
run
dog
jackal
hunt

45
pig
seed
farm
sow
hole

Example
e
f
n
k

46
f
t
r
b

47
s
w
k
f

48
l
r
e
w

49
b
a
g
t

Example
ps
ds
ch
ct

50
ch
th
br
st

51
la
er
sa
he

52
re
se
it
ts

53
ed
gr
be
le

Example
Lions are cruel.
Lions are flesh.
Lions are not stone.
Lions are animals because
they hunt.

CONTINUE

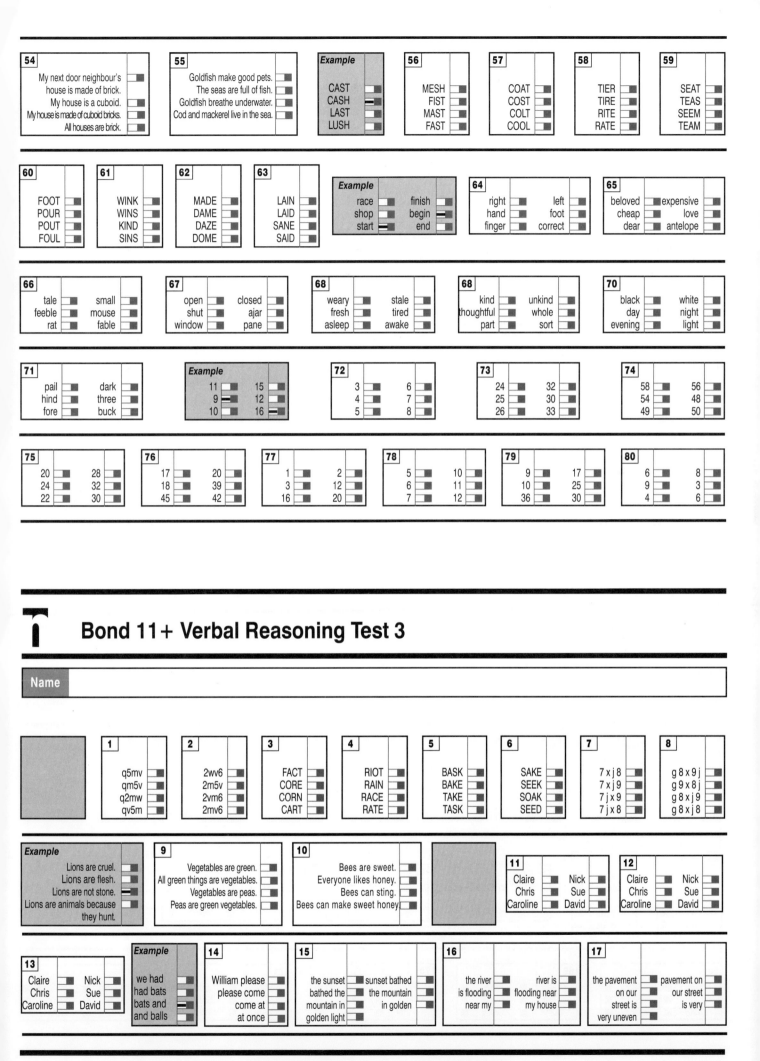

54
My next door neighbour's house is made of brick.
My house is a cuboid.
My house is made of cuboid bricks.
All houses are brick.

55
Goldfish make good pets.
The seas are full of fish.
Goldfish breathe underwater.
Cod and mackerel live in the sea.

Example
CAST
CASH
LAST
LUSH

56
MESH
FIST
MAST
FAST

57
COAT
COST
COLT
COOL

58
TIER
TIRE
RITE
RATE

59
SEAT
TEAS
SEEM
TEAM

60
FOOT
POUR
POUT
FOUL

61
WINK
WINS
KIND
SINS

62
MADE
DAME
DAZE
DOME

63
LAIN
LAID
SANE
SAID

Example
race   finish
shop   begin
start   end

64
right   left
hand   foot
finger   correct

65
beloved   expensive
cheap   love
dear   antelope

66
tale   small
feeble   mouse
rat   fable

67
open   closed
shut   ajar
window   pane

68
weary   stale
fresh   tired
asleep   awake

68
kind   unkind
thoughtful whole
part   sort

70
black   white
day   night
evening   light

71
pail   dark
hind   three
fore   buck

Example
11   15
9   12
10   16

72
3   6
4   7
5   8

73
24   32
25   30
26   33

74
58   56
54   48
49   50

75
20   28
24   32
22   30

76
17   20
18   39
45   42

77
1   2
3   12
16   20

78
5   10
6   11
7   12

79
9   17
10   25
36   30

80
6   8
9   3
4   6

Bond 11+ Verbal Reasoning Test 3

Name

1
q5mv
qm5v
q2mw
qv5m

2
2wv6
2m5v
2vm6
2mv6

3
FACT
CORE
CORN
CART

4
RIOT
RAIN
RACE
RATE

5
BASK
BAKE
TAKE
TASK

6
SAKE
SEEK
SOAK
SEED

7
7 x j 8
7 x j 9
7 j x 9
7 j x 8

8
g 8 x 9 j
g 9 x 8 j
g 8 x j 9
g 8 x j 8

Example
Lions are cruel.
Lions are flesh.
Lions are not stone.
Lions are animals because they hunt.

9
Vegetables are green.
All green things are vegetables.
Vegetables are peas.
Peas are green vegetables.

10
Bees are sweet.
Everyone likes honey.
Bees can sting.
Bees can make sweet honey.

11
Claire   Nick
Chris   Sue
Caroline   David

12
Claire   Nick
Chris   Sue
Caroline   David

13
Claire   Nick
Chris   Sue
Caroline   David

Example
we had
had bats
bats and
and balls

14
William please
please come
come at
at once

15
the sunset   sunset bathed
bathed the   the mountain
mountain in   in golden
golden light

16
the river   river is
is flooding   flooding near
near my   my house

17
the pavement   pavement on
on our   our street
street is   is very
very uneven

CONTINUE TO THE NEXT PAGE

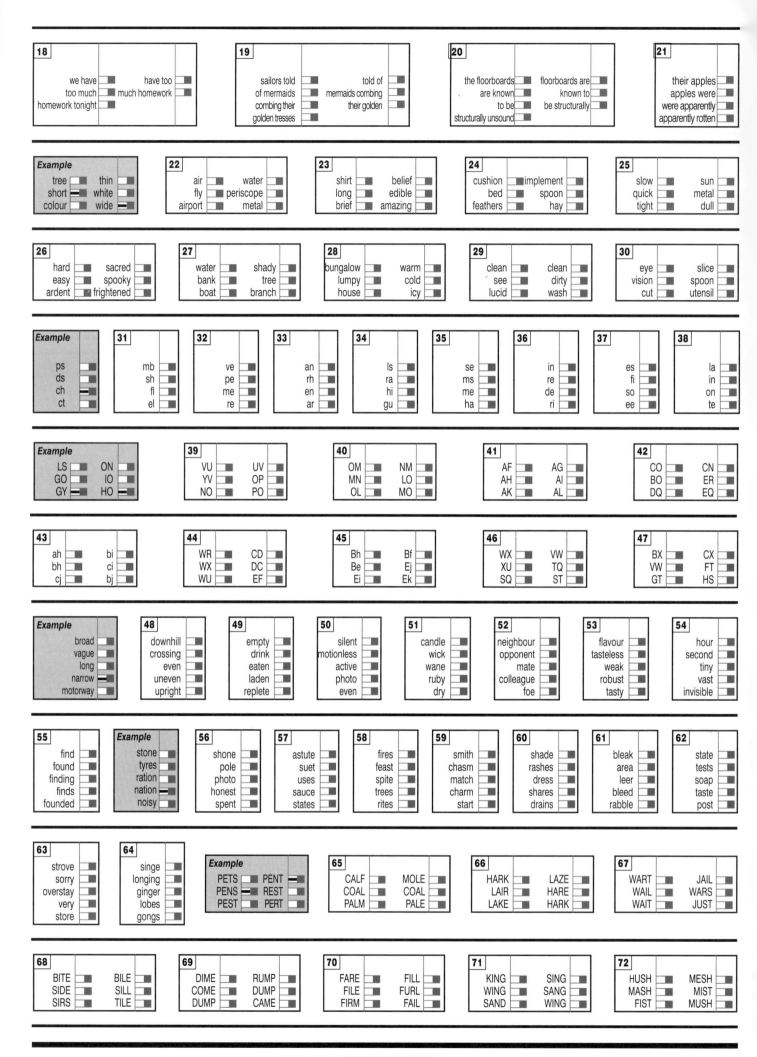

18
we have | have too
too much | much homework
homework tonight

19
sailors told | told of
of mermaids | mermaids combing
combing their | their golden
golden tresses

20
the floorboards | floorboards are
are known | known to
to be | be structurally
structurally unsound

21
their apples
apples were
were apparently
apparently rotten

Example
tree | thin
short | white
colour | wide

22
air | water
fly | periscope
airport | metal

23
shirt | belief
long | edible
brief | amazing

24
cushion | implement
bed | spoon
feathers | hay

25
slow | sun
quick | metal
tight | dull

26
hard | sacred
easy | spooky
ardent | frightened

27
water | shady
bank | tree
boat | branch

28
bungalow | warm
lumpy | cold
house | icy

29
clean | clean
see | dirty
lucid | wash

30
eye | slice
vision | spoon
cut | utensil

Example
ps
ds
ch
ct

31
mb
sh
fl
el

32
ve
pe
me
re

33
an
rh
en
ar

34
ls
ra
hi
gu

35
se
ms
me
ha

36
in
re
de
ri

37
es
fi
so
ee

38
la
in
on
te

Example
LS | ON
GO | IO
GY | HO

39
VU | UV
YV | OP
NO | PO

40
OM | NM
MN | LO
OL | MO

41
AF | AG
AH | AI
AK | AL

42
CO | CN
BO | ER
DQ | EQ

43
ah | bi
bh | ci
cj | bj

44
WR | CD
WX | DC
WU | EF

45
Bh | Bf
Be | Ej
Ei | Ek

46
WX | VW
XU | TQ
SQ | ST

47
BX | CX
VW | FT
GT | HS

Example
broad
vague
long
narrow
motorway

48
downhill
crossing
even
uneven
upright

49
empty
drink
eaten
laden
replete

50
silent
motionless
active
photo
even

51
candle
wick
wane
ruby
dry

52
neighbour
opponent
mate
colleague
foe

53
flavour
tasteless
weak
robust
tasty

54
hour
second
tiny
vast
invisible

55
find
found
finding
finds
founded

Example
stone
tyres
ration
nation
noisy

56
shone
pole
photo
honest
spent

57
astute
suet
uses
sauce
states

58
fires
feast
spite
trees
rites

59
smith
chasm
match
charm
start

60
shade
rashes
dress
shares
drains

61
bleak
area
leer
bleed
rabble

62
state
tests
soap
taste
post

63
strove
sorry
overstay
very
store

64
singe
longing
ginger
lobes
gongs

Example
PETS | PENT
PENS | REST
PEST | PERT

65
CALF | MOLE
COAL | COAL
PALM | PALE

66
HARK | LAZE
LAIR | HARE
LAKE | HARK

67
WART | JAIL
WAIL | WARS
WAIT | JUST

68
BITE | BILE
SIDE | SILL
SIRS | TILE

69
DIME | RUMP
COME | DUMP
DUMP | CAME

70
FARE | FILL
FILE | FURL
FIRM | FAIL

71
KING | SING
WING | SANG
SAND | WING

72
HUSH | MESH
MASH | MIST
FIST | MUSH

CONTINUE

73		74		75		76		77		78		79		80	
11		12		21		21		19		20		22		25	
13		10		18		19		17		21		21		20	
14		11		20		20		16		22		20		22	
9		9		17		22		18		19		23		24	

Bond 11+ Verbal Reasoning Test 4

Name

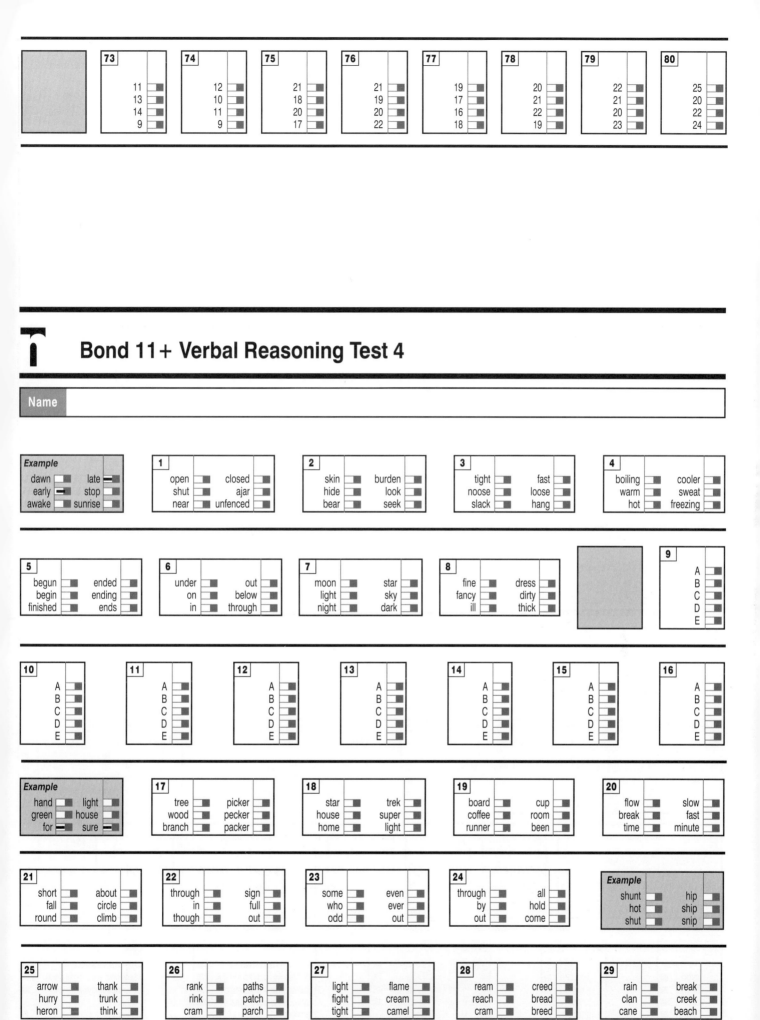

Example

dawn	late
early	stop
awake	sunrise

1

open	closed
shut	ajar
near	unfenced

2

skin	burden
hide	look
bear	seek

3

tight	fast
noose	loose
slack	hang

4

boiling	cooler
warm	sweat
hot	freezing

5

begun	ended
begin	ending
finished	ends

6

under	out
on	below
in	through

7

moon	star
light	sky
night	dark

8

fine	dress
fancy	dirty
ill	thick

9

A
B
C
D
E

10

A
B
C
D
E

11

A
B
C
D
E

12

A
B
C
D
E

13

A
B
C
D
E

14

A
B
C
D
E

15

A
B
C
D
E

16

A
B
C
D
E

Example

hand	light
green	house
for	sure

17

tree	picker
wood	pecker
branch	packer

18

star	trek
house	super
home	light

19

board	cup
coffee	room
runner	been

20

flow	slow
break	fast
time	minute

21

short	about
fall	circle
round	climb

22

through	sign
in	full
though	out

23

some	even
who	ever
odd	out

24

through	all
by	hold
out	come

Example

shunt	hip
hot	ship
shut	snip

25

arrow	thank
hurry	trunk
heron	think

26

rank	paths
rink	patch
cram	parch

27

light	flame
fight	cream
tight	camel

28

ream	creed
reach	bread
cram	breed

29

rain	break
clan	creek
cane	beach

CONTINUE TO THE NEXT PAGE

30
toes		hens	
hose		then	
hoes		hone	

31
trough		frog	
tough		flog	
though		thug	

32
bat		music	
oat		bemuse	
boa		mouse	

33
tray		hovers	
star		hooves	
arts		hem	

34
one		five	
two		six	
three		seven	
four		eight	

35
1		5	
2		6	
3		7	
4		8	

36
1		5	
2		6	
3		7	
4		8	

Example
PETS		PENT	
PENS		REST	
PEST		PERT	

37
TALE		HILT	
MALT		SILT	
SALT		TILT	

38
HOPE		HARE	
HARD		HIRE	
HARE		HEAR	

39
SUEZ		SUIT	
QUIT		SEAT	
QUIN		DUET	

40
STEM		SEEM	
SOUP		SEEP	
STEP		SEAM	

41
PINT		WIND	
WINK		WAIL	
WINE		WANT	

42
CARS		CARS	
SCAR		CUTE	
CURS		CART	

43
POST		MARK	
MAST		PARK	
PAST		PORT	

44
FARM		POLE	
FILE		PILE	
FEEL		PALE	

Example
price	
hasten	
strike	
charge	
money	

45
scene	
part	
leave	
school	
sum	

46
shell	
tide	
recognise	
see	
wave	

47
price	
dear	
sweet	
cheap	
kind	

48
possess	
ore	
mine	
belong	
pit	

49
stick	
leaf	
tree	
tack	
mend	

50
second	
examine	
tell	
follow	
watch	

51
bridle	
groom	
jump	
hat	
bell	

52
dustbin	
lorry	
tip	
litter	
table	

53
may	
gun	
spring	
boot	
march	

Example
11		15	
9		12	
10		16	

54
20		23	
18		24	
22		21	

55
55		35	
50		30	
48		28	

56
25		40	
30		50	
20		60	

57
18		33	
20		18	
33		20	

58
71		61	
13		71	
15		13	

59
3		48	
6		72	
8		36	

60
32		6	
30		33	
3		20	

61
8		8	
16		16	
32		32	

62
4		12	
8		10	
16		8	

Example
we had	
had bats	
bats and	
and balls	

63
dates can		can be	
be found		found on	
on palm		palm trees	

64
please attach		attach your	
your pencils		pencils to	
to your		your clipboards	

65
the small		small boy	
boy lost		lost his	
his mother		mother in	
in the		the crowd	

66
Tom's spectacular		spectacular save	
save ensured		ensured victory	
victory for		for the	
the home		home side	

67
waves tumbled		tumbled and	
and crashed		crashed on	
on the		the shingle	

68
the cheetah		cheetah can	
can reach		reach incredible	
incredible speeds		speeds over	
over short		short distances	

69
an old		old man	
man fell		fell on	
on the		the ice	
ice and		and broke	
broke his		his hip	

70
Amy wanted		wanted to	
to sit		sit in	
in the		the row	
row in		in front	
front of		of Neil	

71
g s p l	
g p s l	
g s l p	
p g s l	

72
t q q p o	
t t p q o	
t q p p o	
t q p o o	

73
KNITS	
KNOWN	
KNIFE	
KNEEL	

74
SAWING	
SALADS	
SAUNAS	
SAUCER	

75
TONG	
TOMB	
TOUR	
TOME	

76
GRAVEL	
GORGON	
GROUND	
GROUPS	

77
cyprf	
cpyrf	
cypfr	
bzprf	

78
jumcqr	
jmucrq	
jumcrq	
jmucqr	

Example
Lions are cruel.	
Lions are flesh.	
Lions are not stone.	
Lions are animals because they hunt.	

79
Shoes are worn with socks.	
All shoes are made from leather.	
Leather shoes are waterproof.	
Leather is the best material for shoes.	

80
All words are written.	
Sentences are made of words.	
letters are always written with a pen.	
Words can be written.	